DAILY REFLECTIONS

365 Days of
Contemplation
for Mind & Soul

By

Robert N. Jacobs

Grosvenor House
Publishing Limited

This book is published by
Grosvenor House Publishing Ltd
Link House
140 The Broadway, Tolworth, Surrey, KT6 7HT.
www.grosvenorhousepublishing.co.uk

A CIP record for this book
is available from the British Library

ISBN 978-1-80381-164-2

To my beautiful daughter, Ava Aurora Skye.
May the words in this book inspire you as much as
you inspired me to write them.
You still inspire me every day!

"Reflective thinking turns experience into insight."

John C. Maxwell.

Foreword

"Change comes from reflection."

Genesis P-Orridge.

It's New Year's Eve, and I have been spending some time in reflection. It's the perfect time of year to look back and reflect on what you've done right over the year and to learn from all you've done.

On further consideration, I've realised that the habit of reflection is something I've developed quite strongly this year. It's actually one of the secrets to my successes. At least once a day, and often several times a day, I reflect on my day, on my life, on what I've been doing right, and on what's not working.

I reflect on every aspect of my life, and from this habit of reflection, I'm able to continuously improve. Reflection gave me the topic of this book and the daily narratives that follow. Reflection also gives me the focus I need to keep on making improvements in all I do and in all I am.

If you haven't already, I highly recommend that you develop the daily habit of reflection in your own way. You may find it brings profound change into your life.

Here are just a few inspirational benefits of reflection:

1. It helps you learn from your mistakes.

If we don't reflect on our mistakes, we're doomed to repeat them – and there's not a lot of wisdom in that. However, if you reflect on mistakes made, figure out what went wrong, look at how you might prevent them from happening again, then mistakes are a means of getting better. Far from being something to feel embarrassed or upset about, mistakes are valuable learning tools. Reflection helps you to see the lessons and learn from them.

2. It gives you great ideas.

Every narrative in this book has come from my daily reflections: reflections on where I am in my life, what is going right, what is going wrong, lessons I can learn, and steps I can take to improve my standards. In short, I reflect on the philosophy and spirituality of my life. I reflect on the things I'm doing or the things going on in my life.

If things are not going well, I'm learning things from it that I can share with others, and if things are going well, I reflect on where that success has come from, and I share that too. Ideas come from reflection, and I've had many this year.

3. It helps you help others.

The ideas I have aren't just things I feel like writing about, they are ways that I can share what I've learned. In sharing, I can help others going through similar experiences, and in the past year I've learned just how powerful this can be. I began the year with the hope that some of the things I've learned in the past year or two might be helpful to others, and I'm ending the year with the profound realisation that simple little tips can help change people's lives for the better.

4. It makes you happier.

Reflecting on the things you did right allows you to celebrate your successes, no matter how small. You're reminded of the positives, and everything you've achieved in life that you should celebrate. Without positive reflection in this way, it's all too easy to slip into focusing only on your failures – and there's no happiness in that.

5. It gives perspective.

In the busyness of daily life, the feeling of overwhelm is increasingly common. A high-pressure lifestyle, whether it's trying to meet tight deadlines or simply trying to be all things to all people, can lead to a setback or a mistake becoming the proverbial straw that breaks the camel's back. In reflection, you gain an opportunity to step back and see the bigger picture. In the grand scheme of things, are the "end of the world" problems you're facing really insurmountable? In reflection, you find calm, and in calm you see things from a different perspective.

How to Get the Most from Daily Reflections.

If reflection is something you haven't, up until now, taken the time to do often enough, consider making it a habit – something you do every day, just like brushing your teeth.

Here are some suggestions that may help you achieve this:

1. Focus on doing it at the same time, every day. No exceptions. Get into the reflection habit by taking just a few minutes at the start or end of every day to read the day's reflection point. Journaling can help to crystalise those reflections.

2. Never skip a day. When you travel, take your *Daily Reflections* book with you. Try not to break the habit of daily reflection, just as you'd try not to let life get in the way of brushing your teeth! Your *Daily Reflections* book is not just for one year, think of it as your daily reflection tool for life. Make it a daily appointment you have with

yourself, and you'll soon realise that reflection time is not a chore, it's something to enjoy.

3.   Think about your day, your work, your life – in that order. I like to reflect on my day, think about what I did right and wrong, and what could be improved. Then I take a look at my work, see how things are going there, then I step even further back and take a look at my life as a whole. It's a three-step system that leads to a lot of improvement over time.

4.   Lastly, you may or may not agree with some, or any, of the reflection points in this book. That is OK. The beauty of contemplating and reflecting on an idea is that you come to your own conclusions and therefore build your own beliefs. This is the ultimate purpose of daily reflection.

It was Germany Kent who famously said – "Take time daily to reflect on how much you have. It may not be all that you want, but remember someone somewhere is dreaming to have what you have." And on that positive note, let's begin...

Robert Jacobs

Curious By Design

January 1st

You can't control what other people do, you can only control what you do – and how you react to what others do – so creating change in your world begins and ends with creating change in yourself. As someone wise once said, "Be the change you want to see in the world." Instead of wasting energy being angry at the world and frustrated by the actions of others, turn your attention to your own thoughts and actions and consider how they influence the world around you.

Are you living your life in a way that betters your world, or are you unwittingly getting in your own way by remaining enslaved to outside influences? Your ego, keeping up with the Joneses, winning the approval of others, and chasing material aspirations are all follies that prevent you from achieving a life and a world that truly matters.

Aspire to rise above the pressures of society and choose to live a more meaningful life.

Don't aspire to be better than the other person, but aspire to be better than your previous self.

'First things first' is a commonly used expression, but saying it and doing it are two different things. It means putting work before play, doing what needs to be done before what's more fun to do, and putting the needs of others before your own. These things should be first, but in a selfish world full of distractions, it's not always an easy rule to stick by.

Getting off to a good start and putting first things first will take you halfway to success in whatever it is you're doing. Think of a 100-metre sprinter on a race start line: if a bad start is made, the race is probably lost. Think of a new business venture: if false claims are made at the start, the poor reputation earned is going to be tough to shake off. When you apply this thinking to all other areas of life, you realise that starting as you mean to go on is key to achieving what you want.

To achieve a successful life that is also simple, beautiful and peaceful, a good start is to set out with a selfless purpose, the positive intent to do the right thing by others, a strong moral compass, and an honest and trustworthy attitude in everything you do. Putting first things first will lead to good things following in their wake.

———◈———

The innermost self will always feel the loss of decency, integrity, and goodness.

Consider what matters most to you right now, and then consider if you are at peace with this reality. If not, consider what changes you could make to better your world and create a ripple effect that positively influences the world at large.

January 3rd

Is it possible to have too much of a good thing? There can be little doubt that many will believe the answer to be no, but many others will have come to the realisation that what they thought they needed to be happy was not what they needed at all. When the 'good things' are selfish needs, materialistic in nature or designed to provide instant gratification, the novelty can soon wear off, and all that's left is a sense of something missing in life. Filling the gap is aspiring to *be* more, not *have* more.

Choosing to be the best version of you it's possible to be is the first step towards becoming that person. The choice is always yours to make. True happiness comes from within and finding it begins and ends with seeking ways to be better and do better in every thought and every action in daily life.

To find inner peace, let pride and ego go.

Anything you can imagine can be achieved.

January 4th

The more you want to achieve something, the more likely it is that you will. Thinking that achieving something might be a nice idea is far less powerful than wanting to achieve something and committing to making it happen.

Instead of setting your mind to believing that something won't happen, set your thoughts to believing that it can happen. Until you believe it's possible, it remains impossible for you. The thoughts and opinions of others are immaterial; self-belief is all that matters. Believing it can happen is the beginning of making it happen.

───────◈───────

What you think about, you bring about. Your thoughts influence your actions, and your actions impact your outcomes in life.

Good things can happen. Success is possible.

January 5th

The door to a higher place is always open; the only thing preventing you from stepping through is yourself. If you've resigned yourself to the life you have rather than the life you want, you're holding yourself back – it's your choice.

The good things in life are just as available as the bad things in life, and you always have a choice. You can choose to focus on the negatives and let life get you down, or you can choose to find the positives that also exist in every outcome, then use them as stepping-stones to lead you through that open door.

———◇———

What you believe to be true is true for you,
so believe in your ability to achieve.

There's no such thing as a good or bad choice,
there's only choice, and there's always another to be made.

January 6th

To never be tempted is an unrealistic expectation. Instead, finding a way to overcome temptations as they inevitably arise is a more realistic aspiration. 'When the going gets tough, the tough get going' may be a truism for many, but no one is immune to moments of weakness when temptation can sneak in and chip away at even the strongest resolve.

Understanding temptation is the most effective way to overcome it. In effect, it's knowing your enemy, but it's also knowing yourself. Pay attention to the moments when giving in to it is all too easy and look for ways to avoid those situations. The more you know, the more prepared you are to deal with it. Be proactive and take control before temptation controls you.

───────◈───────

*Today's choice may be different to yesterday's choice;
always remain open to changing your mind.*

Take time out each day to reflect on what truly matters to you.

January 7th

To move from where you are to where you want to be in life, you must be prepared to leave what's no longer needed behind. Letting go is simply making space for growth. To make way for new knowledge and understanding, you need to clear away old and redundant thoughts and habits that are cluttering your life.

Until you let go of the belief that you can't achieve the life you want, you block your path to achieving it. Until you abandon old habits that stand in the way of making the changes you want, new habits can't become established.

Think of letting go as the price you must pay to have more of the life you want. Clearing a space for new and better thoughts and habits to become established is the only way to break free of the old for good, allowing you to move onwards and upwards without looking back.

As distractions and sources of temptation become clear,
take action to distance yourself from them.

Aim high and commit to letting go of
everything that holds you back.

It's not the person you show to the outer world that matters, it's who you are as a person on the inside. Who you are at heart is the real you. Doing a good deed for someone or saying something nice to someone doesn't make you a good or nice person if you are inwardly resenting the action or words.

Outwardly trying to be someone you're not can only ever lead to meaningful change if your inner thoughts match your outer actions. If they don't, you're only kidding yourself.

No one is perfect, and no one can get everything right every time. Accepting your flaws and taking responsibility for your mistakes is the only way to learn from them and do better next time. Blaming your shortcomings on others, or everything other than yourself, will prevent you from ever experiencing true and genuine change for the better.

Without selfishness and clinging on to what we don't need, the world would be a better place for all.

Your thoughts and actions are always your responsibility, no one else's.

January 9th

There are always positives to be found in every outcome, even failure. It doesn't feel good at the time, but failure is nothing more than feedback. Cliché as it sounds, failure really is an opportunity to learn.

Once the disappointment is over, reflecting on the experience and evaluating what went right as well as what went wrong is a powerful way to pick up the pieces, move on, and do better next time. By taking the positives and the lessons learned forward with you, you're in a much stronger position to achieve the outcome you want.

Taking responsibility for mistakes made is an essential element of learning, improving, and then moving on. Blaming others for failures in your own actions can only ever keep you stuck where you are, destined to repeat the same mistakes and fail again.

It takes strength of character to remain true to yourself, and even greater strength to accept personal responsibility for weaknesses.

The greater the challenge, the greater the victory in overcoming it.

January 10th

To make changes for the better in your life, you need to make space for those better things. Unless you clear out the old, there's limited room for the new to come in. Think of a kitchen cupboard crammed full of unhealthy snacks. If the change you want to make is to switch to a healthier diet, you need to clear out the cupboard to make space for healthier options. If you leave the unhealthy options in there, there's no room – and you leave yourself wide open to temptation.

Clearing space and removing temptation can be applied to all areas of life. If your mind is full of anger, hatred, and negativity, there's no room for positive change until you *make* space. The more space you make, the more positivity you allow in, and the more changes for the better you're able to experience.

———◆———

Taking personal responsibility and doing the right thing is at the heart of being better and doing better.

No one is perfect, but being your best self and doing your best (for yourself and others) each day is living a good life.

Success is a journey. Achieving a goal should always be considered as a springboard to achieving the next rather than an end in itself. To be the best version of you it's possible to be, each positive change made needs to be maintained. If it's your goal to lose a certain amount of weight, achieving this goal is only the beginning. To maintain the new weight, the new habits that led to achieving it need to be maintained.

To be better and do better in any aspect of life, positive changes made need to be maintained. Outward changes are only the beginning, it's the inner changes you make that matter. If it's your goal to build your self-belief, outwardly saying you believe in yourself can only ever have a temporary effect if inwardly you are doubting the truth in those words. Change must come from within – you must *be* the changes you make in every thought and every action.

———◈———

What you think you have or don't have in life is only ever your perception.

Your outer world can only ever be a reflection of your inner world; you are what you believe you are.

In life, just as in sport, champions are made, not born. You already have everything you need to achieve your true potential in life; all it takes is the ability to recognise and practice the skills and habits that will allow you to step up to the next level.

Champions recognise the champion within. Champions believe in themselves as champions in the making at every stage of their journey. Not every day's training will go to plan, and not every competition will be won, but champions in the making never lose sight of what's yet to come. They turn their attention to what can be done to do better next time.

Losing a game doesn't make *you* a loser; having a bad day doesn't make *you* bad; failing to achieve a goal doesn't make *you* a failure. Each new day is another opportunity to develop your strengths and improve on your weaknesses.

Your true potential can be realised; all it takes is a willingness to keep your focus on what *can* still be achieved with dedicated effort and practice, not what has already happened and can no longer be changed. The thoughts and actions of yesterday have gone, you can't change them, but you have total control over the thoughts and actions of tomorrow.

Make your goal a daily affirmation. Say it and believe it. Write it down and keep it nearby so that it can act as a powerful reminder should temptation strike.

Your true potential can only be achieved through focused action.

January 13th

Who you are today does not determine who you can be tomorrow, and your circumstances on any given day do not define who you are. Each new day is an opportunity to be better and do better.

Each new day is an opportunity to abandon negative thoughts and patterns of behaviour that hold you back and prevent you from becoming who you want to be. With each new day, you have the opportunity to make changes for the better, and the way you choose to think and act each day is always your choice to make.

Champions in life don't dwell on negatives,
they focus on finding the positives.

Choose to be your best self; choose to be honest,
genuine, and always true to yourself.

There's no such thing as an overnight success. There's no magic wand that can be waved to take you from where you are to where you want to be. To succeed, you must prepare to succeed, create a plan of action, and then move towards your goal one small successful step at a time.

Snowdrops can appear to spring from nowhere into bloom overnight, but reaching the point of bursting into flower has been an ongoing process of growth. A musician can appear to leap from being a complete unknown to being a top-selling artist overnight, but their success is the result of many years of preparation for success and being ready to grab their opportunity when it came.

Preparing for success also means preparing for failure. Success won't come to you, you must go to it, so you must be prepared to overcome obstacles that threaten to block your path. Each challenge overcome is confirmation of your determination to succeed, and each small success is another stepping-stone that takes you closer to your goal.

Start each new day with the intention of doing good and doing no harm – this applies to yourself and others.

Keep your mind focused on your goal, and then every thought and action will keep you moving towards it.

January 15th

Sadness can feel like a dark rain cloud hanging over you, but consider this: without rain, crops can't grow. Just as rain is an essential element in life, so is sadness. In the same way that rain promotes the growth of crops, sadness promotes the growth of you as an individual.

Everything in life has a natural cycle. Each year is a cycle of seasons. Rain will come and rain will go: sunshine will return. Sadness will also come and go, and happiness will return. Like a rain cloud, sadness will also clear away.

Times of sadness provide moments of reflection. Experiencing sadness equips you with empathy to help others through tough times, and reflecting on the cause of sadness can help you to grow in knowledge and understanding of yourself. Most importantly, it creates an opportunity to consider the effects of your words and actions on other people.

Dark days will pass, and the light days ahead are waiting to welcome you.

Thinking of others helps to push your own dark clouds away.

January 16th

Happiness is a life filled with good thoughts, positive actions, and meaningful employment. Positive thoughts generate positive emotions, and those emotions fuel positive behaviours that in turn promote the overall feel-good factor that keeps the positive cycle repeating.

Of course, negative happenings are part of life, and negative thoughts and emotions will accompany them, but with a mind focused on finding positives, those negatives are prevented from taking up residence and dragging you down.

Unhappiness and negativity can only enter your mind and take over your life if you choose to make space and invite them in. Keeping your life filled with positives leaves no room for negativity to make more than a passing visit.

───────◆◆◆───────

Live your life in a way that's considerate and respectful of others.

Happiness comes from within and from being your best self.

January 17th

Worrying about the future is counterproductive. You can't know for sure what's going to happen in the future, but you can influence what happens tomorrow with your thoughts and actions today. This means living in the present is a much more productive approach.

What you think and what you do today will impact the outcome of your tomorrow. There can be no guarantees, but positive thoughts and positive actions will have a positive influence, just as negativity will have a negative influence. Instead of worrying about what may or may not happen in the weeks, months, or years to come, concern yourself only with the here and now.

Be your best self in the present moment and make every thought and every action count as a positive step on your journey towards being the best it's possible to be. Living in the moment frees you from the worry of an unknown future.

***

All things in life are governed by the law of cause and effect: your thoughts govern your outcomes.

When you think good thoughts and do good things, good things will come to you.

January 18th

Knowing who you are, believing in who you are, and remaining true to yourself at all times is the way to weather any storm. A storm may be facing opposition or criticism, it may be a local dispute or global unrest, it may be a conflict with others or within yourself, but weathering it comes down to trusting and remaining steadfast in your values.

Inner peace comes from trusting in yourself to do the right thing and quietly standing by your principles. Knowing who you are and what matters most to you makes you someone whose actions speak louder than words and someone others can believe in. Lasting peace comes from having no grudges to bear and no hatred for others to carry around: peace is letting go of any past wrongs and being free of any bitterness.

Always be authentic; be genuine in all you say and do.

If there's conflict and hate in your heart for others, there can be no inner peace.

January 19th

Just as there's no point in attempting to repair storm damage while the storm is still raging, there's no point in attempting to make decisions or changes while you're raging with anger or in the midst of any emotional storm. Nature has a way of creating a stillness after a storm, a momentary calmness and quietness in which every living creature appears to pause and take stock, and you should do the same.

After the emotional storm has passed, take a moment to pause and reflect. It's in this quiet, calm time that everything can be put into perspective. What seemed like an insurmountable mountain may reveal itself to be a molehill, and actions or words that angered you may be seen in a different and kinder light. The heat of the moment is not the time to make decisions or take actions. Let the storm subside. Then, in the calm of reflection, see things as they really are and allow your thoughts and actions to reflect the real you and what really matters to you.

Letting go can be painful, but going through discomfort is necessary if you are to become free of it.

It's often in the depths of sorrow that what matters most becomes clear.

January 20th

Everyone experiences heartache and sadness at some point in life. When it happens to you, you are never alone. Sorrow is simply part of what it means to be human. When your tears are flowing, keep in mind that the tears of many others around the world will also be flowing. You have not been singled out; you are not alone in your experience of pain. Use this understanding to feel greater compassion for others and to lift yourself out of self-pity.

Sadness will pass and happiness will return. Everything in life is on a sliding spectrum. If there was no sadness, there could be no happiness. It's part of the human condition to experience your share of both.

———◈———

Make every thought and action a reflection of the best version of you.

Sorrow will end and joy will follow.

January 21st

Life moves in cycles. Just as the seasons change, daylight follows darkness, tides ebb and flow, and calm follows a storm, times of sadness will return to times of gladness, and joy will return after pain.

Accepting these natural cycles and flowing with them is the quickest and easiest way to get through them. Imagine an athlete facing the pain of injury and the prospect of not being fit to compete in a major competition. Fighting against the natural cycle of recovery will only lead to further injury, prolonging their return to fitness. It's like swimming against the tide.

Choosing to flow with the tide rather than fight it is choosing to let go of anger, frustration, and negative thinking, making space for the positive thinking that will promote recovery. Know that these cycles are part of life, and know that by flowing with them you will return from pain to joy, and the joy you return to will be far greater. Sometimes, the real value of something is not realised until it's taken away from you.

Through sorrow, you discover what it is to be without sorrow. Unless you know sadness, you can't know joy.

Tides will continue to turn. Knowing what truly matters allows you to return to the shore without getting caught in the turbulent waves of what doesn't matter.

January 22nd

In happiness and unhappiness, in joy and sorrow, in success and failure, in victory and defeat, in work and play, the determining factor in each and all of these circumstances in life is character. In every individual's character lie the hidden causes of every outward happening in their life.

Character is both cause and effect. It is the doer of deeds and the recipient of results. A negative character will experience negative outcomes; a positive character will experience positive outcomes. Your character shapes your life, and you can shape your character.

Wisdom is clearing away all selfish traits and establishing a positive character.

In choosing to find a way over, through or around all difficulties, you choose to stay on course to achieving what matters.

January 23rd

When difficulties arise in life, you can choose to give in and be beaten back or you can choose to find a way around them. Challenges come in all shapes and sizes, from niggling problems to huge obstacles that block your path, but there's no challenge so great that it can't be overcome. Finding a way through, over, or around it may take time, and it may require deep thought and physical effort, but every difficulty is simply a test of your strength and resolve.

The tougher the test, the greater your sense of achievement when you pass it. Every difficulty overcome, no matter how small, is a reminder of your determination to succeed; each victory is a reminder that you *can* find a way.

When you believe in yourself, and your every thought and action back up your belief, nothing can stand in your way in life.

There's no difficulty that can't be overcome when you choose to look to yourself, not others, to find the answer.

January 24th

Success is rarely the result of a one-off action; it requires repeated action. An athlete can only become stronger by exercising and training their muscles with repeated and progressive efforts, and the same principle can be applied to mental as well as physical achievements.

If you want to know more, you need to learn more; if you want to master a skill, you need to practice more; if you want to be better and do better, you need to be prepared to be more and do more.

Hard work and effort are not something to shy away from when the discipline of repeating those efforts will lead you to the success you want.

There's no difficulty that can't be overcome when you choose to look to yourself, not others, to find the answer.

To achieve what you want, you must do what needs to be done.

January 25th

When things go wrong, getting mad or upset about it changes nothing. In fact, it only makes things worse. As the saying goes, there's no point in crying over spilt milk. Just as you can't put the milk back into the bottle, you can't undo something that has already been done. Whatever it is that has gone wrong, making a huge fuss over it won't make it go right.

Things *are* going to go wrong in life. Plans will get derailed, and obstacles will block your path. That's life. When you choose to develop a positive mental attitude, you are able to deal with setbacks much more calmly and constructively. Without the added drama, you free yourself from the vicious downward spiral of negative thinking, and you can move on. The sooner you move on, the sooner you can make things go right.

To succeed, you need to commit to doing what it takes for as long as it takes. There's no shortcut to success.

A calm mind is a constructive mind. Negativity is clutter.

Believing that happiness can be found in material possessions is flawed thinking. Stories of unhappy millionaires are all too common. Having a bigger house, a faster car, or more money in the bank may create an illusion of happiness, but it can only ever be temporary. True happiness and lasting happiness comes from within.

Until you are happy just being who you are, true happiness will never be yours. If you believe that having someone else's life or someone else's appearance would make you happy, you're sadly mistaken. You would only ever be temporarily satisfied with what you have, and you would always want more. True happiness is found in what you have left when all external trappings are stripped away. Happiness is who you are, not what you have.

With a positive mental attitude, a drama-free route out of a crisis can always be found.

According to the law of cause and effect, your thoughts are the cause, and your life is the effect.

January 27th

Nature is never in a hurry. No shortcuts are ever taken, and no makeshift time-saving alternatives are ever used to replace natural processes. Everything in nature comes and goes in its own good time, and patience is rewarded with perfect beauty.

Compare this to the impatience of most people in life. One minute late is fussed over as a huge inconvenience; goods out of stock or delayed in transit leads to outrage, and instant is never fast enough. All of this hurry and impatience generates a world of discontent and disappointment. Take a moment to stop and realise the ridiculousness of rushing through life. What perfect beauty does it bring?

Someone wise once said, "There's no shortcut to any place worth going." Success is a journey, so make sure it's a place worth going by taking the time to enjoy the ride.

Your experiences in life grow into wisdom, and wisdom blossoms into peace and happiness.

Impatience is a waste of time. Instead, make good use of each minute as it comes and goes, and what you need will come to you.

January 28th

When your goal seems a long way away, remember that every positive action you take is a step closer. Even on the coldest and darkest of days, you have no doubt that warm, bright days are ahead. Never doubt that the good things you want are just ahead.

Just as all living things in nature continue to prepare for the season ahead, never doubting or questioning its arrival, remain certain in your thoughts and actions that every effort you make is bringing your goal closer to you. When you live each day in a meaningful way that betters the world around you, your summer will come.

———◦◦◦◦◦◦———

Unselfish thoughts and deeds will always lead to beautiful outcomes, and those outcomes will inspire more of the same.

When your heart is in everything you do, no task is a chore.

Without sadness, there can be no happiness; without low, there can be no high, and without fast, there can be no slow. Everything in life is relevant to something else, including success and failure. Realising this helps you to keep all of life's ups and downs in perspective.

The experience of setbacks or failure is necessary if you are to experience success. As Winston Churchill once said, "Success is not final, failure is not fatal: it is the courage to continue that counts." By adopting this attitude, you accept that mistakes or failures are not the end of the road for you, and something positive and useful can always be learned from them.

Failure in your eyes may be success in someone else's – it's all relative – and in understanding this, you realise that you have the power to change your circumstances by changing your perspective.

Just as dark days become light, negativity can be overcome to allow positivity in. Change is always possible.

In the school of life, experience is the teacher. Far more is gained from learning with patience and humility than from sulking in the back of the class.

What you think about, you bring about. In other words, focusing on everything you don't like in your life will bring more of it into your life – and vice versa. To have more of what you want, you must focus your thoughts on having those things.

To be better and do better, you must think and act as the best version of you, and believe in yourself as that person. With thoughts focused on influencing your world in a positive way and all thoughts of selfishness cleared from your mind, what you bring about will be what truly matters in life.

———✦———

Shift the focus of your thoughts, prayers, and meditations to the good you want to see in your world and use the positive energy generated to make it your reality.

The secret to becoming more than you are; is to think and believe that you can become more than you are.

If it's change you want, what you say must match what you think and what you do before any change can take place. Saying you want to lose weight but always thinking you'll start your diet tomorrow and continuing to eat in the same way as before will not lead to weight loss.

Saying that you want to earn the respect of others but then failing to show respect for others in your thoughts and actions will not earn you what you want. Saying you want to make a change for the better but then allowing your thoughts to return to the old way and making no change in the way you do things will make any lasting change impossible. To change, you must think and act as if the change has already taken place.

If you keep your thoughts focused on being the best version of you it's possible to be, you will surely become your best self.

Keep your thoughts on what you want, not what you don't want.

February 1st

Can true happiness ever be found? Is finding inner peace just a pipe dream? There is a way to find both. To know happiness, you need to understand the root of your unhappiness, and to know peace, you need to understand what it is that prevents you from feeling it.

Until you accept and understand these things, any move towards finding happiness and peace can only be temporary. Denying the existence of thoughts and behaviours that lead to unhappiness and unrest can only ever keep you stuck in a loop that you're destined to repeat. To reach a place of true happiness and peace, you must first understand the things that pull you back.

———◆———

Pain, sadness, and upset are shadows that follow everyone in life. Being your best self is choosing to turn your face to the sun and keeping those shadows behind you.

There's a lesson to be learned in every experience, even unhappiness.

February 2nd

When you stray from the path that leads to your goal, you must reflect on the thoughts and actions that led to straying. Failure is nothing more than feedback, and it's feedback that allows you to learn.

Mistakes are only ever mistakes if they're repeated without any of the learning applied, and learning can only take place if you're willing to learn. Look to yourself, rather than looking for something else to blame, and use the lesson learned to get you back on track. The more you learn in life, the more you grow.

———◦◆◦———

Understanding what you don't want is part of discovering what you do want.

Your thoughts and actions are your responsibility, and you are responsible for what they bring into your life.

February 3rd

All that you are is all that you have experienced in life. Your experience of life is individual to you, and for this reason, your view of the world is different to another's view. The more you remain open to new experiences, the more you will know, and the greater your opportunity to gain new perspectives.

Your thoughts and your inner view of the world influence your view of the outer world. In other words, your attitude influences your outcomes in life. If your thoughts are negative, you're only going to see negativity that confirms those thoughts, and you'll remain blinkered to everything positive. In effect, your thoughts are self-fulfilling prophecies.

What you choose to be on the inside is what your world will be on the outside.

Every thought and every experience you have in life makes you who you are. Changing your thoughts and experiencing new things can change who you are.

February 4th

'Man has no enemy greater than himself' is a famous quote that can be applied to many aspects of life, not least selfishness. If you're going through life only looking out for No.1, you are indeed your own worst enemy. In fact, with this attitude, everyone around you is your enemy, and you have no room for friends.

It's only by choosing to adopt a selfless attitude that you can experience the love and joy of friendship and all the positive things it brings into your life. By opening your heart to others, you have nothing to lose and everything to gain.

———⸭⸭⸭⸭———

Good things will always be found by those who look for them.

The good things in life are already there, they're just waiting for you to find them.

February 5th

To find good in the world, you need to believe that there is good to be found. To be better and do better in life, you need to believe in the better version of you. Adjusting the filter through which you view the world allows you to see all the positives you may have become blinkered to, and adjusting your thoughts allows you to see beyond where you are to where you want to be and can be. The life you live is the life you believe in.

———◆———

Whatever you can imagine, you can create.

You have to believe it to achieve it.

February 6th

The mind is a powerful force. There's nothing that can't be achieved when all thoughts and actions remain focused on achieving it. Thinking positively allows you to find another way when challenges block your path. Also, believing in your ability to achieve directs all your positive energy into doing whatever it takes to succeed.

However, this power can only be effective when positive thoughts and actions are maintained. Negative thinking holds the same power. If you believe no other way can be found, your path will remain blocked, and if you believe you don't have what it takes to achieve, you won't succeed.

Every thought is energy. The energy in your environment, good or bad, is under your control, and your energy influences everyone around you.

———◆———

As the saying goes, you can achieve whatever you put your mind to, and nothing can stand in the way of positive intention and unshakeable faith.

Thinking good thoughts will bring good things into your life.

Be aware of the company you keep. Just as the energy of positive people rubs off on those around them, so does the energy of negative people. Misery loves company. Getting caught up in the negative emotions of doom and gloom merchants can sap your energy and drag you down. Distancing yourself from these influences means being prepared to stand alone.

Be a mighty oak rather than a willowy reed; be a solid rock rather than shifting sand. Be someone who knows who they are and what they believe in rather than someone who bends and shifts to the will of outside influences. As someone wise once said, "You become who you associate with."

———◈———

Until you are in control of your own thoughts and actions, you must consider the control your thoughts and actions may have over others.

Know your own mind and be unshakeable in your beliefs.

February 8th

Getting what you want in life should never be at the expense of others. Doing the right thing by yourself and by others is the only way to truly prosper. Competition can lead to the belief that "nice guys always finish last", and the only way to succeed is to be ruthless at best and dishonest at worst. Those who choose to behave this way would do well to remember that what goes up must come down.

Be better and do better. Gains made at the expense of others will never be gains that can be enjoyed without fear of losing them to some other ruthless individual. Only by doing the right thing can any gains made bring true prosperity into your life.

Be who you want to be, not who others want you to be.
Always be true to yourself.

Always do what you believe to be the right thing to do; trust your best self, and you won't go far wrong.

February 9th

Whatever you put your mind to can happen for you, and when your heart is in it, things happen with ease. When your positive thoughts and actions are genuine, the positive energy they generate will keep you moving forwards towards your goal *and* bring the things you need to achieve it towards you.

Authenticity is key. With both heart and mind intent on achieving an authentic and meaningful purpose, there's no room for doubt. Every thought and every action is effortlessly moving you closer.

Power over your own thoughts and actions is perfect power.

Authenticity is truth. Knowing the true you is true wisdom.

February 10th

There's a distinct difference between meditation and daydreaming. In a daydream, your thoughts might wander in any direction, and they might be pure flights of fantasy that serve no real purpose, but in meditation, your thoughts become focused on sifting through the clutter of your mind and pinpointing what really matters in your life.

The purpose of meditation is not to dwell on negatives but to clear space for positives. Dwelling on past injustices or grudges, or reliving every "woe is me" moment of self-pity can only keep you trapped in a negative frame of mind. Until you let go of those thoughts, there's little room for new thoughts to enter and a positive frame of mind to develop.

In meditation, sort through your thoughts and choose to let go of those that are only holding you back. Clear space for new learning, new growth, and new ideas to blossom.

———⋄———

If you are genuine in your want for something, you will be willing to do whatever it takes to achieve it.

Let the purpose of meditation be finding what truly matters and clearing away what doesn't.

February 11th

The word 'want' has power. Compare wanting to achieve something
to thinking it might be a nice idea to achieve something.
Wanting adds a sense of commitment to making it happen.

When this is applied to meditation, the want must be to stay
focused on what matters to you and to avoid drifting into a fanciful
daydream or slipping into a negative cycle of thoughts. To do this
takes self-discipline. With self-discipline, you can steer your thoughts
in a purposeful direction. Without self-discipline, you are a straw
drifting aimlessly on the ocean of life.

―――――◈――――――

*Open your mind daily to receive inspiration, just as a flower opens its
petals to receive the morning light.*

*Dare to dream big; have high aspirations, and soar fearlessly towards
them on the wings of self-belief.*

February 12th

If you follow a path from its start point, you're eventually going to come to its end point. Wherever there's a beginning, there's going to be an end. Of course, there are right starts and wrong starts, so the way something begins impacts the way it ends.

Making a wrong start is effectively going to lead you down the wrong path, whereas making a right start is going to help lead you to where you want to go. However, if you're to get to the end point you want, you must start as you mean to go on.

Give careful consideration to the way you begin each new day. Make it a right start, and make sure it's the way you mean to go on.

———◈◈◈———

In line with the theory of cause and effect, a beginning is a cause and what follows next is the effect.

The effect will always follow suit with the cause.
Good endings follow right starts.

February 13th

Everything in the universe is made of tiny particles. The perfection in each of these tiny particles creates perfection in the bigger things they make. If just one tiny detail is flawed, the whole it creates is flawed. If just one tiny particle were to be missed out, the whole would no longer exist.

In life, every tiny detail matters. Every thought and every action, no matter how tiny, is a part of the whole you're creating. No one is perfect, but being your best and doing your best in every moment of every day is building perfection into your world and the life you want – one brick at a time.

Wisdom is found in the everyday details of everyday life.

When each composite part is the best it can be, the whole they create will be the best it can be.

'Don't put off until tomorrow what can be done today' is an old and familiar proverb. The message it contains for many is that putting things off will generally lead to those things never getting done at all, but the key lesson in the words is that nothing can happen unless you're prepared to *make* it happen. It's a message of doing rather than thinking, and getting on with what needs to be done to achieve what you want.

Making things happen means not only paying attention to the big things in life but also the thousand-and-one little things that need to be done on a daily basis. Doing each little thing in turn and doing each one to the best of your ability establishes a positive habit of making things happen. Doing, and doing well, keeps you moving forwards every day.

Neglecting small tasks or not doing them to the best of your ability shows a lack of commitment.

It's what you do in the present moment that keeps you on track to achieving what you want in the next.

February 15th

What you say is of no value if it's not what you do. Telling others how they should live their lives is meaningless if it's not how you live yours. Thinking that small discrepancies, little indulgences, and little white lies are of no consequence is flawed thinking. Unless your actions match your words, you lose all credibility. Telling yourself that you're definitely sticking to your diet this time and then indulging in an extra piece of cake every day instantly cancels out your words, and this applies to every aspect of life.

Every little thing you do matters, not just the big things. Every thought you have influences every action you take. If you think the little things are of no consequence, then you have lost the power to influence the outcome of bigger things. To be better and do better, you must be your best and do your best in everything you do, every day. As the saying goes: 'If you take care of the pennies, the pounds will take care of themselves.'

If you take care of the little things, you will achieve great things.

Consider the consequences of every small discrepancy. Only by matching your actions to your words in every small thing can you achieve any goal, big or small.

February 16th

Who you are as a person is determined by who you are in each thought and each action you take. Your overall character is the sum of many small details. To be deemed a generous character, every small act of kindness and every small selfless thought has added up to create the impression of who you are as a whole.

To be deemed an honest character, honesty must be evident in every small detail of your life, and to be deemed trustworthy, you must be true to your word in everything you say and everything you do. You become who you are through the small details, and in choosing to be and do your best in each one, you become your best self.

Who you are is evident in every tiny detail.

Thoroughness in all you do adds up to the best you.

February 17th

The way you see the world can be very different to the way someone else sees the world. What you perceive to be real can be very different to someone else's perception of reality. Your opinion of an event can be very different to the opinion of someone else who witnessed the same event.

Everything you see in your world is being filtered through your beliefs and past experiences. If you're looking for negatives, you'll find them. If you want to find positives, you need to look for them. To find the truth, you need to be able to clear your own filters and be open to seeing a different view.

The true you is not how you're described; it's how you live.

The more thoughtful and considerate you are of different viewpoints, the more opportunities you have to find the truth.

February 18th

Are your thoughts full of envy, suspicion, anger, or hate, or are your thoughts focused on pushing such negativity from your mind? If the former, those things will become your world, and if the latter, you are paving the way to a better world. A life of envy or suspicion is a life of constantly looking over your shoulder, a life of looking out for No.1.

Are you out for yourself, or are you out to better your life and the lives of others? A better life is an unselfish life. When you free yourself from the chains of getting ahead and staying ahead, you are no longer a slave to yourself. You are free to be better, do better, and become your best self, making your world and the world of those around you a better place to be.

The real truth is a truth shared by everyone. See a truth that matters.

Becoming your best self becomes clear to all around you.

February 19th

Temptation is all around, and being tempted is simply being human. It's generally considered a distraction, a bad thing that leads you astray, making it something that should be avoided. However, temptation can be a good thing. Aspiring to be your best self means aspiring to be more than you currently are, so be tempted by the better things you aspire to have.

When you look at it this way, temptation can be a positive motivator. If you're not tempted by anything, you're not aspiring to have or be anything more than you are. If you want to be more, use the power of temptation to keep you on track to being more.

The things that tempt you are the things you think you want. Change your thinking to change your temptations.

The sky is the limit when you aspire to greater things.

February 20th

Change can make you uncomfortable, and the temptation to return to old ways of thinking and doing can be tough to resist. However, recognising an unhelpful temptation is recognising a weakness, and it's only by acknowledging weaknesses that you can develop strengths.

Solutions to problems can only be found once the problem has been recognised, so true strengths can only be found once your weaknesses have been exposed.

The more you know of yourself, the more you understand who you are aspiring to become.

Until you face your flaws, a way to fix them can't be found.

February 21st

Who you are is who you are on the inside. Changing your life on the outside can't change who you are if you're still thinking of the old life on the inside. No longer being a slave to fashion and the latest trends may be a noticeable change on the outside, but if your thoughts are still focused on what you've given up and what you're missing, there has been no change on the inside.

Until your thinking is a match for your doing, the things you do and the words you say remain hollow and meaningless.

———◈———

Finding a better way and becoming a better you requires perseverance.

Giving up the pretence of change is the only way to create true change; be truthful.

February 22nd

Knowing what you value and what matters most in life makes any sacrifice that must be made to achieve it much easier to bear. When you discover the principles that you are prepared to stand by in life, you have all you need to always do the right thing.

A strongly held principle is a powerful thing, and an unchanging principle gives you something solid to hold on to in an ever-changing world.

———————

Letting go in your every thought as well as your every action is letting go of all that holds you back; let go, and you are free to move on.

A life built on a solid principle is indestructible.

February 23rd

A principle only has power if it's never abandoned. If what you say you believe in and are prepared to stand by only applies when things are going your way, and you drop your belief the moment things change, you're no longer a person of principle.

It's only when you're prepared to stand by a principle, no matter how much pressure you come under, that you can benefit from its power to guide you through uncertain times.

———◆———

There are very few men or women with any real power and influence.

Power comes from within. Acquiring it comes down to knowing what you truly believe in, and then standing by it is never in doubt.

February 24th

In a busy world and busy life, it's easy to forget that quiet time and time to reflect is needed to fully recharge your batteries. The buzz of daily life and the energy of being around other people can create an illusion of an energised world, but the activities that appear to give you energy will also steal it away from you unless you take time out away from the busyness to be silent.

Fear of missing out and the distraction of technology can lead to being permanently switched on, but every distraction can only ever offer a temporary top-up. To fully recharge, you need quiet time in which you can just be still and be in the moment.

Stillness offers time for self-reflection and time to reconnect with what really matters. Just as talking less and listening more can help build deeper, more meaningful connections with others, quiet meditation and stillness can help to build a deeper understanding of yourself and a more meaningful connection with your world.

———◆◇◆———

Unhappiness is a reminder that you're being starved of what you want in life. What you aspire to have is the food you need.

It's in time spent alone that the true you can be discovered.

February 25th

What values and principles are at the heart of who you are and what you do? To be your best self, you need to know what it means. Quiet time spent in reflection is valuable time spent reconnecting with what matters most and what doing the right thing in life means to you.

The more deeply you understand the values you hold dear, the easier it becomes to apply them to all aspects of your life – in everything you think, say, and do and in every interaction you have with others.

Knowing what it looks like and feels like to be your best self allows you to identify the shortcomings or weaknesses you need to address to become that person. Knowing and understanding what changes you need to make is the first step towards making those changes happen.

―――――◈――――――

Finding the true you is finding your inner power; your spiritual power.

Know what it means to be your best self and never settle for less.

February 26th

Just as rest is needed to stay physically well, quiet and restful times are needed to boost your mental wellbeing. Good health is health in mind, body, and spirit, and downtime is to your mind what sleep is to your body.

Regular physical activity and rest allow your body to stay strong, and regular time spent in quiet reflection allows you to gather strength in your understanding of what matters most and what you need to let go of.

In an ever-changing world, identifying or reconnecting with unchanging guiding principles keeps you firmly rooted in what really matters.

———————————

In quiet time spent alone, the strength to meet life's challenges can be found.

To really know yourself and understand what matters to you in life, you need to spend time alone.

February 27th

You can't make the entire world a better place on your own, but you can make your world a better place. If everyone in the world shared the same approach, a better world for all would be achieved. Being better and doing better becomes easier when you feel that you belong to something bigger than yourself.

The value of doing your best by everyone becomes instantly clear when you understand that your thoughts and actions influence the thoughts and actions of those you come into contact with. The ripple effect of treating others as you would wish to be treated yourself can change your world for the better.

Make what you need a reflection of what the world needs.

Doing the right thing becomes the only thing when you are part of something bigger than yourself.

February 28th

When you learn how to be comfortable in your own company, you learn how to find peace. If being by yourself makes you uncomfortable, how can you ever be truly comfortable in the company of others? If quiet time alone with your own thoughts is something you try to avoid, what escape is there from those same thoughts when you're with others? Everything outside of yourself is in a constant state of change.

Relationships and friendships can come and go, jobs and social situations can change, and people can move away. Until you get comfortable with your own thoughts and find peace in spending time alone, there's no security in your world. Peace and security must always come from within.

Always stand by what you know to be the right thing.

Learn to enjoy your own company and you will never be alone.

February 29th

Until you know your own mind and the guiding principles you will always stand by, you will never know true freedom. If you depend on the approval of others to feel secure in your choices, you will forever be insecure.

It's only when you become secure in who you are and what matters most to you – irrespective of the opinion of others – that you can find true freedom. Independent thought is freedom, and self-reliance is security, but this becomes meaningless if you slip into considering yourself better than others. True freedom is found in having no need to compare yourself to others and in trusting yourself to always be and do your best.

Know who you are and know what matters, and you have what you need to stand alone.

When you free yourself from the need of another's approval, true freedom and peace can be yours.

March 1st

Your attitude to life has a huge impact on the life you live. What you believe influences your thoughts, and the way you think influences the way you feel. The way you feel and your attitude to life then influences your behaviours, and those behaviours then shape the way things turn out for you.

In effect, your thoughts become self-fulfilling prophecies. Clearing the way for a better life begins with clearing away limiting beliefs and attitudes that prevent you from being your best and doing your best. Change on the outside comes from change on the inside.

In the same way that a hidden spring will eventually be revealed above ground, what's hidden in your heart will eventually reveal itself in your life.

Your attitude is your own making. Change is also yours to make.

Choosing to see a better you and a better life is choosing to see possibilities and to believe in those possibilities. What you choose to believe in becomes your reality; such is the power of the mind. Choosing to believe that change is always possible paves the way for positive changes to be made in your life.

Choosing to see yourself as the person you aspire to become makes staying on the path to achieving your goal much simpler. When you believe in yourself as your best self, negative outside influences and distractions hold no power over the positivity in your heart, mind, and actions.

———❖———

There's no greater aspiration than wanting to be your best self.

There is nothing more blissful than choosing to adopt a calm, wise, and positive outlook.

March 3rd

As someone wise once said, "We are what we repeatedly do. Excellence, then, is not an act, but a habit." In other words, excellence isn't found in doing something just once or twice, it's found in doing something regularly and repeatedly. To be able to think positively, you need to be able to hold positive thoughts and images in your mind often enough for positive thinking to become an everyday habit – something you do without giving it any conscious thought.

Just as learning and mastering a physical skill takes time, effort, and dedicated practice, the same applies to learning and mastering a mental skill. A master pianist becomes a master by perfecting every small stage of improvement along the way until excellence at the highest level is achieved. A positive thinker becomes a master of their mind by perfecting every little thought in everyday life until positive thinking becomes a well-established and perfected habit.

———————

The more you repeat a positive thought in your mind, the more thinking positively becomes a habit.

What you feel in your heart is what you see in your world.

March 4th

The life you experience is the outcome of your thoughts and habits. When you understand this, you realise that by changing your thoughts and habits, you can change your life. Freeing your mind of negative thoughts and limiting beliefs and establishing positive habits will allow you to be better and do better, bringing you the outcomes you want in life.

Change is a step-by-step process, and achieving what you want won't happen overnight. Radical changes are rarely sustainable, but small changes made and maintained on a daily basis will take you step-by-step towards the life you want.

All negativity can be overcome.

Truly living your best life is being your best in every thought, word, and action.

March 5th

It's always going to be easier to do what you want to do rather than what you feel you *should* do or have to do, but it's doing everything to the best of your ability that allows you to become the best version of you. If you aspire to be better and do better, *everything* you do to the best of your ability is taking you towards that goal.

When you adopt this attitude, the little tasks or duties that seem to be getting in the way of what you want to do suddenly become a part of getting where you want to be. Consider this: it's not the task itself that's irksome, it's wanting to be somewhere else or doing something else that can make it feel like a chore. There are no chores when every task done well is simply part of becoming your best self.

Until you do everything that must be done to the best of your ability, achieving what you want will remain out of reach.

Always do a good job, and you will always be on track to becoming your best self.

March 6th

There's a saying, "You reap what you sow." In other words, you get out of life what you put in. If life is not giving you what you want, you need to reflect on what you put in. If your focus is always on negatives, and if everything you do is done grudgingly, nothing positive can be received in return.

If your focus is turned instead to looking for positives, and if everything you do is done to the best of your ability, you are opening your mind and your heart to receiving the good things that will come your way. Call it fate or call it destiny, the way life turns out for you is not outwith your control. What you choose to sow is what you will reap: if all you plant is negativity, then all you can grow is more of the same.

You are responsible for all you do and how you choose to do it, so you are responsible for the character you develop.

Your attitude is your destiny: your destiny is your making.

March 7th

Life is a series of lessons, so as a pupil in the school of life, ask yourself what your report card might say. Are you a diligent pupil, learning every lesson and using knowledge to become wiser and happier, or are you messing around in the back of the class, failing to pay attention and remaining unhappy with your lot in life?

Just as being open to learning new things in a classroom will lead to intellectual growth, being open to learning new things in life will lead to personal growth. Until there is a willingness to learn, no learning can take place, and until new ways of thinking and doing are understood, there can be no new outcomes in life.

———————◆◇◆———————

All unhappiness springs from a negative frame of mind.

Happiness is keeping an open heart and mind.

March 8th

If you are too busy finding fault in others, you have no time left to recognise and work on your own flaws. Not only does thinking that everyone else is at fault suggest you're seeing no fault in yourself, it also means that you're in a constant state of annoyance at others.

Until you recognise where there's room for improvement in yourself, no improvements can be made, and it's only by letting go of negative thought processes that you free your mind to focus on the positives that are all around you. Turn your attention away from others and put your energy into thinking your best thoughts, doing your best in all you do, and freeing yourself from negativity.

To find peace, you must break away from negative thoughts and emotions.

The way forward in life is always there if you choose to look for it.

March 9th

Do you have ambitions or aspirations? Having an ambition is generally having a desire to achieve a personal goal – becoming a millionaire or becoming an Olympic athlete – and the same can be said of aspiring to achieve something, but there is a subtle difference. Ambition means there can be no satisfaction until the goal is achieved, whereas aspiring to achieve a goal means that every successful step towards achieving it brings satisfaction in itself.

Both ambition and aspiration are motivational in terms of achieving something, but most importantly of all, both are indicators that you're ready to be more than you currently are. Ambition alone might lead to selfish thoughts and actions, but in choosing an aspirational goal, you're choosing to achieve it in the best way possible by being your best self.

Make it your ambition to be better and do better, but aspire to achieve it in a way that betters your world and the world of all those around you.

———◆◇◆———

Aspiration is seeking to make not only your world a better place but the world of all others around you.

All that you aspire to achieve is possible.

March 10th

Adopting a positive mental attitude may be your goal, but with the best will in the world, maintaining it can be a challenge. Negative thoughts will creep back in from time to time, and things will happen that derail your good intentions, but these setbacks are only temporary. All is not lost.

With aspiration as your guide, you will get back on track, and with each step you take, you are renewing your commitment to developing a positive mental attitude and establishing new, positive habits.

———◈◈◈◈———

Aspiration sets you on the right path to becoming your best self.

Refresh and renew your mind each day with thoughts of all you aspire to achieve.

March 11th

Attitudes and mindsets can be changed. A negative outlook on life can become a positive outlook, and it takes no more energy to think positively than it does to dwell on negatives. The law of Conservation of Energy states that energy cannot be created or destroyed, it can only be transferred from one type to another.

When you apply this formula to everyday life, you realise that switching the way you think and behave to adopt new and better habits doesn't require a whole new source of energy. You already have all the energy you need as soon as you switch your focus from everything that hasn't gone your way in life to everything that can and will go your way as you become your best self.

———◇◈◇———

Reflection allows all that's unimportant to be sifted away, leaving only what truly matters to shine through.

Switching your focus is like clearing the clouds from the sky.

March 12th

On the journey from where you are to where you want to be, there's going to be a midway point where thoughts of turning back will mix with thoughts of moving on and never looking back. This is only natural. It's that point in your journey where old habits need to be abandoned completely, and giving up everything that's familiar can feel like a sacrifice that's too big to make.

By turning thoughts of sacrifice into thoughts of creation instead, you realise that the familiar things you're loathed to part with are being cleared away to make space for new and better things to come your way.

Familiar feels comfortable, unfamiliar feels uncomfortable, but the new and different habits you're creating will soon become as familiar and comfortable as the old ones, only this time they're better – they are the "new and improved recipe" – and they are going to help create the new and improved you.

Change can be uncomfortable, but changes for the better soon bring all the comfort you need.

Get comfortable with uncomfortable and the greater comforts of peace and love will become yours.

March 13th

To be the bigger person is to be the better person. To be able to love when faced with hate, to be able to rise above resentments, and to be able to do so without complaining is being the bigger person. As the better person, you don't try to argue your point or convince others of their mistakes; you simply do what you know to be the right thing to do in every situation.

When your thoughts are right, right actions will follow, and calmly doing what needs to be done and doing it to the best of your ability will help to bring calm into the world around you.

All of your yesterdays have created your today. Who you are today is the result of your every thought and every action in the past.

The way that you habitual think and act becomes your character.

Nothing in life happens without a reason. This is not to say that bad things don't happen to good people, but in the grand scale of things, the way things go for you in life will be the result of the way you think and act in life.

If you are putting positive effort into achieving a certain outcome, you will achieve it. If you are half-heartedly wishing you could achieve a certain outcome, you won't achieve it. Every thought and every action becomes a reason. To achieve the life you want, you need to ensure there's no reason why you shouldn't.

―――――◈―――――

Whatever your version of heaven and hell, they are in this world.

The school of life is where character is developed.

March 15th

Humans are creatures of habit, and habits are often described as habits of a lifetime. They become who you are and what you do, and you often don't even remember when they started – they're subconscious. Just as old habits began as repeated thoughts or actions, so can new habits begin.

Pay attention to the thoughts that enter your mind and make a conscious effort to ensure all negativity is moved on. Make it a daily practice to clear away all negativity, and soon the positive thoughts that remain will enter your subconscious – they are now who you are and what you do.

Changing your thoughts can change what's in your heart.

Good thoughts generate good actions. Make every thought good and you become as you think.

March 16th

Your life is as you think it is, and you are responsible for your thoughts. This means that all that makes you happy and all that makes you miserable in life is also your responsibility. Positive thoughts don't hold magical powers, but they do have the power to bring the things you want into your life.

If you want to be better and do better in life, you must believe in yourself as the person you're becoming, and the positive actions that will take you there will follow from those positive thoughts. If you choose to wallow in self-pity and misery, believing that nothing in life ever goes your way, those negative thoughts have equal power – nothing will go your way.

———◆◇◆———

Your thoughts and emotions are under your control.

Calmness is found in choosing positivity over negativity. There's only drama in your life if you look for it.

March 17th

"God, grant me the serenity to accept the things I cannot change, courage to change the things I can, and wisdom to know the difference." These words are the Serenity Prayer written by Reinhold Niebuhr, but they're also wise words commonly quoted in popular culture.

Life is full of challenges, and these include difficult people as well as difficult situations. You have no control over the thoughts and actions of others, so having the serenity to accept the things you cannot change definitely applies here. No matter how annoying you find another's point of view, getting into an argument over it only drags you into a negative state of mind.

Rather than trying to prove your point in a war of words and then continuing to live in a state of annoyance as they refuse to see it, let your actions speak louder than words. Have the courage and the wisdom to make your point through *being* who you are and *doing* what you do. Be your best self, and you'll find peace in place of annoyance.

The more you know, the more you understand.

A life of being your best and doing your best is a life of peace.

March 18th

In today's world of quick fixes, patience is rare. However, just one hour each day devoted to quiet meditation and reflection on what matters most and what it means to be your best self will bring a sense of calm into your world, helping you to keep everything in life in perspective.

Calmness prevents rashness; patience prevents impulsiveness, and reflection acts as a guide, providing the answers to the questions of what it means to be your best self and what it takes to do the right thing. Give meditation and reflection time, and you will be rewarded with the life you want – all in good time.

————◆————

Impatience goes hand-in-hand with impulse, neither of which being helpful in life.

Keep becoming, keep growing, and your mistakes will become fewer as you become better.

March 19th

In a dog-eat-dog world, there can be no winners. In a world where everyone looks out only for themselves and gives no consideration to others, everyone loses. Unless you can show kindness to others, why should others show kindness to you?

Unless you can forgive others, why should anyone forgive you? If you're always trying to get ahead, you're always looking over your shoulder to see who is gaining on you. There's no peace, there's no love, and there's no lasting happiness.

Choose a selfless life over a selfish life; choose kindness, forgiveness, and consideration for others, and you will find a life of peace, love, and lasting happiness.

———————◇———————

Truth can only be found in your heart, not in anything outside of yourself.

The way you choose to treat others will influence the way others choose to treat you.

March 20th

Knowledge is power. The more you know about yourself, the more confidence you have in being your true self. When you know what matters to you and what makes you feel good about being who you are, there's nothing that can lead you away from doing what you know in your heart to be the right thing.

Your true self is the person you aspire to be, the person you are becoming day by day by being better and doing better in every thought and every action. Always be true to the best version of yourself. In times of doubt, instead of asking, "What would Superman do?" trust in yourself and ask, "What would the true me do?"

———◆———

Finding what really matters to you in life is finding the path to wisdom and peace.

While you're chasing trivial, short-lived pleasures, you won't find lifelong joy. Be wise and aim higher.

March 21ˢᵗ

Do you see your troubles as something brought about by your
own doing or the doings of others? It can appear at times that the
actions of others have caused the problems you face, but the way you
think and behave in response to the actions of others is always your
choice to make. If you're troubled, it's your doing. This is simply the
theory of cause and effect. The effect someone else's actions have on
you is under your control, so the cause is not the action, it's your
response to it.

Everything that happens to you, whether it's good or bad,
is brought about by you. For every action, there's a repercussion.
What you do comes back to you. What someone else does comes back
to them. This can be tough to accept at times, but getting caught up in
blaming others or making excuses can only ever keep you stuck in a
negative place.

———❦———

Your suffering is not brought to you through others, only through you.

*You are not the result of your outward conditions; those conditions
are the result of you.*

March 22nd

Wealth, status, and possessions can be mistaken for success, but true success can never be measured by what you have, only by what you are. You might have a life full of luxuries, but if you have gained them by putting yourself before all others, you're not a true success.

You might be living a life of oppression and hardship, but if you stand by your principles and always do the right thing by yourself and others, you are a true success. There's no true success in having more if all it creates is more reason to step on others to get what you want and more reason to look over your shoulder as you live in fear of losing it.

Your circumstances don't define who you are, only your thoughts and actions. Think of it this way: do you want future generations to remember you for what you had, or for who you were? When you think of it this way, you realise that success is not possessions, it's how you make people feel.

There is freedom in knowing what truly matters and in letting everything else go.

When you know in your heart that you are doing the right thing, nothing can drag you down.

March 23rd

Positive thinking is not wearing rose-tinted glasses, it's seeing reality and looking for the positives that can always be found, no matter what the circumstances.

With a positive attitude, anxiety, fear, disappointment, and sadness can all be overcome, because no matter what changes take place in the outside world, there will always be an inner place of calm acceptance and understanding.

Positive thinking provides certainty in uncertain times. Life is change, but knowing yourself, knowing what matters, and being sure of your commitment to always being and doing your best provides a means of overcoming whatever upset comes your way.

———◆◇◆———

Those thinking good thoughts and doing good deeds will always find joy.

Peace will always be found in being true to yourself.

March 24th

A selfish body flatters itself; a selfless spirit gives an honest appraisal.

A selfish body seeks instant gratification; a selfless spirit knows patience and discipline. A selfish body can put up a façade, a fake front; a selfless spirit has no secrets and nothing to hide.

A selfish body holds bitter grudges; a selfless spirit can forgive the bitterest of enemies. A selfish body can be noisy, rude, and inconsiderate of others; a selfless spirit knows silence and graciousness. A selfish body is thoughtless; a selfless spirit is always thoughtful.

———◈———

As a selfless spirit, you will find gentleness, patience, compassion, forgiveness, and love for all in your heart.

Where there's no selfless spirit, you will find hatred, pride, anger, revenge, and cruelty, and the finger of blame always pointed at others.

March 25th

A vision of what it means to be a better you will become clear in your mind before it becomes your reality. Holding that vision takes practice. Change takes time, and it's only by repeating a new pattern of behaviour that it can become the new norm. It's often said that practice makes perfect, but this is only helpful if what you're practising is perfect.

Repeatedly doing something badly will only lead to becoming perfect at doing that something badly. Holding a vision of the person you want to become and taking time at the end of each day to reflect on which thoughts and behaviours were a match and which were not makes it possible for you to keep learning, keep adjusting, and keep being and doing better so that your perfect vision becomes your reality.

You can only show others how to be better if you have become better yourself.

Your best self will be known when love is perfected and revealed in all you think and do.

March 26th

Until weaknesses are recognised, improvements can't be made. This is not to say that you should find fault in yourself at every opportunity, it's equally important to recognise strengths, but knowing where there's room for improvement is the first step in making those improvements.

Changes don't need to be dramatic. Small improvements add up to big improvements. Do every daily task to the best of your ability, without thinking of any personal gain; do everything you can to make those around you happy; be kind in what you say, do kind things when you can, and rise above any thoughts of retaliation when others show unkindness around you. Do these things daily, and every day you are becoming your best self.

———◈◈◈———

Follow faithfully the path that leads to being the best version of you it's possible to be.

Put your whole heart into being your best in every minute and every hour of every day.

March 27th

Being your best self and being true to yourself is living a free life. If you're keeping no secrets, you have nothing to hide. If you're telling no lies, you can look others in the eye. If you're being genuine in all you say and do, you are always free to be yourself.

There's nothing to fear when you've done no wrong. There's nothing to be ashamed of when you've deceived no one. There's nothing that can knock you down when you're living life being your best and doing what you know to be the right thing.

When you know you're doing the right thing, no one can make you do differently.

No one can wear you down or upset you when your heart is at peace with all.

March 28th

Indignation at the wrongs you see in the world is undoubtedly preferable to indifference. Caring about the plight of others is demonstrating selflessness, but indignation becomes unnecessary when you choose to demonstrate selflessness in your every thought and every action every day.

Caring is not just what you say or what you choose to protest about, it's what you think, what you do, and who you are. Indignation, however well-intended, is still a negative state of mind. Choosing to show care and compassion in everyday life is choosing to maintain a positive state of mind.

With this attitude, every thought and every act is selfless; you are being the change you want to see in the world. What goes around comes around, and those doing wrong will reap what they sow.

———◆———

It is better to love than to point fingers and condemn.

With compassion, indignation and all other negative emotions no longer influence your actions.

March 29th

What does it mean to be a good person? It's not Disneyfied sentimentality or outward displays of goodness that mark someone out as good, it's who they are on the inside. A good person is good from the inside out. Every thought and action comes from the heart, and they have genuine strength of character – they stand by who they are and what they believe in.

There's no goodness in a kind act carried out for show or for some personal gain. This faux goodness may allow someone to get ahead for a while, but it's not who they really are, and their true colours will eventually be revealed. A truly good person is genuinely selfless in all they think and do, and like a stick of rock, "goodness" remains visible all the way through.

There's nothing noble in choosing to do nothing when the right thing could be done.

A genuinely good person is seen in the way they live their life.

March 30th

Successful leaders lead by example, and true teachers teach by example. Knowledge can be gained from books, and lessons can be learned from the experiences of others, but nothing holds any meaning unless the knowledge and lessons learned are applied to the way you live your life.

When you practice what you preach, you become a shining example of the benefits of living your life in the way you do and of choosing to be your best self. Becoming the person you aspire to be in all you think and all you do will inspire others to be the best they can be, and the circle of positive influence widens.

There's no greater aspiration than goodness.

The overarching aim of all religious and spiritual teachings is to show a better way to live.

March 31st

The rules you choose to live by are often unspoken rules based on your understanding of what's right and what's wrong. It's fair to say that most people share the same understanding, but where people differ is in the extent to which they're prepared to bend those rules. In a world where success is based on what you have rather than who you are, it's all too common for some individuals to slip into believing that certain rules no longer apply to them.

The rules of common decency and kindness towards others should never be bent. If everyone in the world chose to abide by these rules, never bending them to suit themselves, just imagine the positive change it would bring to the world.

As one tiny individual in a global population, you might feel there's little you can do to create a better world, but by choosing to always do the right thing by yourself and by others, you are a positive force for good.

———◆◇◆———

Love can't be found in words alone; it must be lived.

What it means to be good is known in the innermost hearts of everyone.

April 1st

Your happiness or unhappiness in life is in your hands. It's not the responsibility of others to make you happy, and it's not the fault of others when you're unhappy. Your own thoughts and consequent actions are the source of the way you feel – or the way you believe you feel.

To be happy, you need to find what makes you feel happy and do more of that. To be free of unhappiness, you need to find what makes you feel unhappy and avoid doing it. Either way, only *you* can find the answers and only you can take the necessary action.

If you're unhappy with your lot in life, you have everything you need to make changes. Good things will begin to come into your life the moment you take responsibility for finding them, and unhappiness will be pushed aside the moment you choose to make space for those good things.

Your thoughts and your actions become who you are and how you live.

Ask yourself, "Is there a better way?" Then do that.

April 2nd

What you think is what you are. It's impossible to be otherwise.
If your thoughts are full of jealousy and hatred, you are a jealous,
hate-filled person. If your thoughts are full of worry and doubt,
you are an anxious, unconfident person.

What's in your mind is what's in your life; the two are inseparable.
Acknowledging this fact makes it clear that changing your life begins
with changing your thoughts.

Whatever you think, you become.

---

*Your life is how you think and act, and your life can change through
your thoughts and actions.*

April 3rd

Thinking positively and doing your best in everything you do will keep you moving towards being the best version of you it's possible to be. Every positive thought and action brings greater energy and greater power into your life, helping you to turn dreams into realities.

Having high aspirations, meditating and reflecting daily on what you can do better to help you stay on track, and committing to doing whatever it takes for as long as it takes to get to where you want to be will keep lifting you up to the next level. Every day of thinking better thoughts and doing better deeds is a new day of being better and doing better, and a new day of becoming the best you.

Who you are is not fixed; the potential for change is always within you.

Every thought and every experience is a modification of your character.

April 4th

The power of the mind is phenomenal. When negative thoughts creep in, they can hijack your entire day, or even your entire life, until you learn how to overcome them. Understanding that thoughts can be changed is fundamental to switching from negative to positive thinking, but understanding the difference between thoughts that help you and thoughts that hold you back is key to bringing about positive change in your life.

When you have a clear vision of who you are as your best self and how you want to live your life, you have the power to make choices that keep you on track to realising that vision. When you know what truly matters to you, impulsive thoughts can no longer lead you astray or influence your choices.

Knowing what "doing the right thing" means to you gives you the strength to stand firm and overcome any temptation; you have control because your thoughts are focused on who you are becoming.

Choosing wise thoughts and doing wise deeds leads to wisdom.

*Your thoughts determine who you are, how you live,
and all you know.*

April 5th

For every action there's a consequence. The consequence of a poor choice is a poor outcome, but by the same token, the consequence of a good choice is a good outcome. What goes around comes around – if it were possible to escape the consequences of poor thoughts and actions, then not benefitting from good thoughts and actions would also be possible.

This is not the way of the world. Negative energy can only bring negative returns, and positive energy will always bring positive returns. There's no randomness. If you want peace and harmony in your world, then every thought and action must be intent on bringing about those positive returns.

———◈———

Where a universal law exists, it can't be partial. Staying on the right side of it brings happiness, straying onto the wrong side of it brings unhappiness.
There's no fence to sit on in between.

Pain is learning. With learning comes wisdom,
and then no more pain.

What does it mean to have good morals? As the world and society have changed, so have moral standards, so your morals are your standards of behaviour and what you believe to be right or wrong – your personal code of ethics. What do you believe to be acceptable behaviour, and what do you value above all else? Would you never tell a lie, or would you tell a lie to avoid hurting someone's feelings? When you consider these questions, you realise that having good morals is doing the right thing, and the right thing may vary depending on the circumstances.

Your moral compass is your guide, but your aim as a good person is to always treat others as you'd wish to be treated yourself. Should you be honest and tell your host that you didn't enjoy the meal they prepared for you? Is it more acceptable to tell a lie and know that you're doing it, or tell the truth and know that you're hurting someone's feelings? For every action, there's a consequence; good morals help you to make good choices in life *and* do the right thing by others as well as yourself.

When you see the bigger picture, you see what really matters in the grand scale of things.

With wisdom, the right thing to do is always known.

April 7th

Can a leopard change its spots? Yes, it can. What has already been done can't be undone, but what happens next can be changed. You can't change what you did in the past, but you can change what you do in the next moment, which in turn will change your future.

When you understand that changing your thoughts changes your patterns of behaviour, you realise that you can change your life. Who you are is who you choose to be, and by changing the way you think and behave, you begin the process of change from who you currently believe yourself to be to who you aspire to be.

To create a better future, you need to see a better future. When you believe that you can be better and do better, you are embracing the changes you need to make; you are choosing to change for the better in every moment of every day.

———◆———

Choose to rise above all that holds you back and level up in the game of life.

Just as upset and turmoil will be found in a selfish life, peace and serenity will be found in a selfless life.

April 8th

When you are living life as your best self, you're no longer at the mercy of trends, fashions, or changing opinions on what's in and what's out; you are totally comfortable being you as you are. When you free yourself from the pressures of keeping up with the latest "must-haves", you free yourself from a life where your worth is measured against what you have rather than who you are. Consider this: if your worth is what you have, you will never have enough. There will always be something more coming along that you must have...

As your best self, you're able to see that continually striving to have more is a sure-fire way of promoting selfishness and courting feelings of envy or frustration. You're also able to see beyond your immediate world to the world at large, understanding the ridiculousness of selfish, materialistic needs when so many lack what they need to simply survive. You already have all you need to become your best self, and as your best self, you will always have enough.

It's only when you recognise what truly matters that you can see the error in your ways.

Good people create good in the world.

April 9th

Failure is an experience, not a thing in itself. You can experience failure, but that doesn't make *you* a failure. You can make a mistake, but that doesn't mean everything you do will be a mistake. You learn, and you gain what you need to do better next time.

Failures, mistakes, and learning are all part of becoming better, so use each experience to gain greater knowledge and understanding of what you need to do next to achieve the outcome you want.

Not being your best is an experience, not a permanent condition.

When you rise above what you are, you become all you can be.

April 10th

With the benefit of hindsight, it becomes possible to see that everything happens for a reason, and there's something positive to be found in every experience. Of course, it's not always possible to see or accept this at the time of it happening.

However, looking back, the things that didn't go as planned were not the disasters you believed them to be; they were lessons you needed to learn. In realising this, you become better equipped to keep learning and keep progressing, no matter what life throws at you.

There are no "bad" or "good" happenings in life, there's only your perception of those happenings. When you choose to look for the positives and the lessons that can be learned, they will always be found. Should you choose to wallow in self-pity instead, no lessons can be learned, and you are destined to remain stuck where you are.

———◆◇◆———

Things won't always go to plan, but lessons will always be learned.

No one determined to be all they can be gives in at the first obstacle in their path.

April 11th

Ancient Chinese military strategist Sun Tzu once said, "Know yourself and you will win all battles." In more recent times, champion surfer Laird Hamilton said, "Make sure your worst enemy doesn't lie between your two ears." What these wise words make clear is that it's not you against the world in terms of achieving your goal, it's you against the voice inside your head.

If you're fighting the battle of the bulge, your enemy is not the person offering you food, it's the voice inside your head saying, "Go on. Just one more slice of cake won't matter." If you're struggling to stay positive in a certain situation, it's not the situation that's your enemy, it's the voice inside your head saying, "This is a disaster; you're doomed to failure and you should give up now."

Knowing yourself is knowing your strengths and your weaknesses. Controlling your thoughts is controlling your enemy. Finding peace in your mind is finding peace in your world.

Conquering the enemy within is winning the greatest battle of them all.

You may win against one opponent and lose against the next, but taking control of your thoughts is a permanent win.

April 12th

Just as force will often lead to rebellion in times of war, there's nothing to be gained by forcing someone to share your point of view. If it's not something they genuinely believe in, forcing your opinion on them will probably only lead to them rebelling against it even more.

Change must come from the heart. To bring about change in yourself, there can be no conflict between your thoughts, words, and actions. To bring about change in others, the benefits of the change must become something they want for themselves.

The most effective way to achieve this outcome is to be a living example of those benefits. There's no force required when all that being better and doing better brings into your life is clearly evident in your every thought, word, and action. The peace you have found will inspire others to find the same. It will become their heart's desire.

Force will give rise to fear and anger, but love will give rise to peace and reform.

Being good and doing good brings all that's good into your life.

April 13th

It's often said that life is what you make it. This is true, but it's often misconstrued to mean that working hard and saving money will allow you to have more luxuries in life. Having luxuries is promoted as "living the dream", but it's invariably a false promise. Having more leads to wanting more, and the more you have, the more you fear losing it all. There's no true happiness to be found in possessions, but TV advertising will always try to convince you otherwise.

True happiness comes from within. To understand this is to free yourself from the chains of always needing more. There's nothing wrong with having creature comforts, but freeing yourself from selfish wants and desires creates space for the peace and happiness that selfless thoughts and actions will bring into your life. Your life *is* what you make it, but a happy life is never delivered to your door in a cardboard box.

The Beatles famously sang, "All you need is love". Reflecting on these words creates an opportunity to look at your life with fresh eyes.

Know what matters; know what love is, and you have true wisdom.

April 14th

Just as seeds planted in nature may take years to yield a crop, the consequences of your thoughts and actions today may not be instantaneous, but you will reap what you sow.

The life you have today is the consequence of how you've lived your life up until this point. If you have sown seeds of hatred, bitterness, envy, or any other negative emotion, the life you have will reflect this. The same applies to sowing seeds of kindness, compassion, love, and other positive emotions.

This is food for thought. If the metaphorical crop you're harvesting today is failing to provide what you want, you need to consider the seeds that have been sown. Raking away old weeds and planting fresh new seeds may be all that's needed to produce a bumper crop in the form of the life you want.

A world caught up in the selfish pursuit of meaningless pleasures is unable to understand that true happiness is found in selflessness.

The whole world is moving towards the realisation that what's planted today will be reaped by future generations.

April 15th

If your heart is full of hatred, prejudice, and condemnation, there's no room for love or forgiveness. Where there's hatred, there's selfishness; where there's love, there's selflessness.

It's only by rising above selfishness that you can find it in your heart to let go of the hatred and all other negativity that's keeping you blinkered to the good in the world, and only then will you realise the power of love and selflessness, and the positivity it brings into your life.

———◈———

Clearing hatred from your heart not only benefits you but all others.

Let go of hatred and let light into your life.

April 16th

Being your best and doing your best is directly linked to treating others as equals. When you are free of prejudice, there's no looking down on others or feeling looked down on by others – there's no need for pigeonholes or boxes. As your best self, your positive attitude is seen in all you think, say, and do, and you endeavour to extend the same unselfish kindness and consideration to all you connect with in your world and the world at large.

Only those with good in their heart see the good in the world.

When all you think and do is selfless, you will be at peace.

April 17th

An impartial mind, compassionate heart, and the ability to bite your tongue rather than argue will give you all you need to win the hearts and minds of others. With a calm and positive attitude, others will believe in you as the real deal. Without any thought of trying to convert others, the merits of your positive thoughts and actions will be clear to see.

Without any need to preach from your soap box, you will teach others a better way by simply being and doing your best at all times, and without any ambition or thoughts of personal gain, you will earn respect and admiration for just being who you are and doing what you do.

With authenticity, genuine love is found.

Doing all you can to help all you can is selfless love.

April 18th

Have you ever been unable to see the wood for the trees? There can be times when you get so caught up in the unimportant details of something that you're no longer paying attention to or even seeing the most important parts of it. When you're caught up in selfish pursuits, you might easily lose sight of what really matters.

When you're caught up in what you have or what you don't have compared to others, you're failing to see that these fixations are unimportant. When you're caught up in petty squabbles or long-standing grudges, it's even possible to forget what caused the upset in the first place.

Realising that you're caught up in unimportant details is opening your eyes and seeing the wood – the bigger picture. Realising that what you have is not who you are, and that who you are is all that matters, can be a revelation, but it can set you on a path to finding true happiness in life.

Instead of sleepwalking through life, doing as others do and being who others believe you to be or want you to be; choose to wake up to being who you want to be, doing what you want to do, and finding what matters most to you.

Open your heart and mind as well as your eyes to see what really matters.

Seeing the truth and realising its beauty is bliss.

April 19th

Until there's certainty in who you are and what matters most to you, it's all too easy to be led astray. You may not be aware of straying onto the wrong path at the time, because until you know where you want to go, you can't be sure of how to get there. Without certainty, you're likely to experience happiness one moment, sadness the next, confidence one day, and fear the next simply because you lack direction in life.

When you pause, reflect, and get to the truth of who you want to be, you gain certainty. Knowing who you are and where you are in life, and getting clear on who you want to become and where you want to get to, gives you direction. Then, understanding what matters most to you gives you all you need to stay on track. No bump in the road can set you off course when you are safe and secure in your knowledge of the real you and your true destination.

———◆◇◆———

Switch uncertainty for certainty, and illusion for reality.

Knowing who you are becoming is turning a light on in your mind.

April 20th

What you know in your heart to be true will never fail you.
The truth for you is constant and dependable, no matter what changes
or upheavals you face in life. Tough challenges may at times cause
you to question what you believe, but the truth will always prevail
when your beliefs are genuine.

A positive and firmly held belief is like a loyal friend, a comforter in
times of discomfort, and a calm voice of support in times of difficulty.
Stand firm in what you believe, and you will always find your truth to
be steadfast and unchangeable in a changeable world.

Knowing what matters is a constant comfort.

---

*Being true to yourself at all times helps to clear away clouds
and let the sunshine through.*

April 21st

The truth for you is what matters most. Your truth is what you believe in; it's your means of sorting right from wrong and your guide to doing the right thing. Knowing what matters most can help you to make good choices in even the toughest of times.

Knowing what doing the right thing truly means can help you to push aside any vain thoughts or selfish acts, and in being your best and doing your best in all you do, you can find peace in your heart and mind.

———◆———

Selfish delusions prevent you from seeing the truth and doing the right thing.

The stronger your belief, the greater your comfort.

April 22nd

There's no hiding from wrong-thinking and wrongdoing. You might think that angry thoughts or acts carried out with less than the best of intentions can be concealed, glossed over, and forgotten, but they will follow you, and they will always catch up with you.

Negativity in your thoughts and behaviours brings negativity into your reality. By the same token, kind thoughts and good deeds done will also follow you. Positivity in your thoughts and behaviours will bring positivity into your reality. When you understand and reflect on this, you realise that by always doing the right thing, you have nothing to hide from. Only good can follow right-thinking and right-doing.

Do no wrong, and you will always have peace in your heart.

The fastest route to where you want to go is the path of least resistance.

April 23rd

Knowledge and wisdom can never be gained through reading alone. Inner peace can never be found through studying the teachings of others alone.

True knowledge will be found in your heart, wisdom in always doing the right thing, and peace in knowing that you are always being and doing your best.

———◈———

With a positive outlook and love in your heart, all sadness will pass like a morning mist.

Love, peace, and wisdom will come into the lives of all who keep choosing to do the right thing.

April 24th

In troubled and dark times, it's not unusual to slip into thinking that there will never be light at the end of the tunnel. Dark thoughts create a negative frame of mind in which it becomes impossible to see anything other than happenings that confirm your mood.

To be able to see the light, you must believe that it is there: to come out of darkness, you must be willing to let light in. Letting go of negative thoughts is the beginning of adopting a more positive frame of mind. Where negative thinking generates a defeatist attitude, positive thinking makes it possible to see things differently.

Until you're looking for a way through or around your difficulties, a way out can't be found. What you believe to be true *is* true for you, so believing you're trapped *will* keep you trapped. To reach the light at the end of the tunnel, you must first believe it's there, and then you must have faith in your ability to get there.

———◈———

Have faith in your ability to overcome, and you will overcome.

To see it, you must believe it.

April 25th

Self-control, self-reliance, and watchfulness will lead you to being the best you can be. Taking control of your thoughts, taking personal responsibility for the actions they generate, and continuing to reflect on every thought and action every day will give you all you need to remain steadfast, patient, and gentle in all you say and do.

With these traits, you have what it takes to always be your best and do your best; you have the power to realise your true potential.

Have faith in all you know, and all you need will come to you.

You have all you need to move closer to your goal every day.

April 26th

Greed and selfishness can only ever bring misery into your life. Instant gratification, luxurious possessions, and looking out for No.1 might bring momentary happiness, but it's an illusion. Having more leads to wanting more, and more will never be enough. If all that you are is what you have or what you can buy, there's no true happiness.

When all that you value is within you, true happiness is yours. When you know in your heart what matters most to you, and you live up to those values, you have no need for material things to bring you happiness – happiness is you. In good times or bad, in success or failure, and in every stage of life, your happiness remains within and can never leave you.

———◇———

Be determined, be patient, and be purposeful.

Let love guide your every thought and action.

April 27th

In the lyrics of 'Imagine', John Lennon sings of being a dreamer, and in today's world, it's a dream that seems far from reality, but just imagine if the dream of love and peace could be a reality in your world.

When you choose to abandon all prejudice and treat everyone with the same care and compassion, you are creating love and peace in your world. When you choose not to argue, retaliate, or carry around resentments, you are creating an inner world of love and peace that will become evident in your outer world.

You may be a dreamer, but you are a dreamer prepared to be and do all you can to turn that dream into a reality. As Lawrence of Arabia once said, "The dreamers of the day are dangerous, for they may act their dream with open eyes, to make it possible."

———◆———

Imagine all you can be, and then be all you imagine.

Be thoughtful, be wise, and be kind.

April 28th

When you no longer put yourself before others, you will find peace in your world. When you consider the impact of your words and actions on others and do all you can for others without any thought of personal gain, you will find peace in your world. When you treat all others as equals and do the right thing by every living thing, peace will always be yours.

When inner peace is yours, you're no longer swayed by external influences; you're no longer caught up in changing trends, you are always true to who you are, and you are always able to see things as they really are.

It's not about you; it's about what you can do for others.

See the good in you and see the good in the world.

April 29th

Without challenges in life, there would be no opportunity to grow. With every problem faced and every setback overcome, you become wiser and stronger. In a growth mindset, you understand that changes for the better can always be made and that who you are now is not set in stone.

When you choose to look for positives, you will always find them, and every positive lesson learned is another step towards becoming your best self.

Until you look, no better way will be found.

Good, better, best. Never let it rest until the good is better, and the better is best.

April 30th

With wisdom comes self-control. Without self-control, you're at the mercy of your emotions, and words spoken or decisions made in the heat of the moment are not always the best.

With wisdom, you're no longer a slave to the ups and downs of moods or fits of temper; you are calm, in control, and able to see things as they really are – not skewed by emotional outbursts.

With self-control, you are the master of your mind, and words spoken or decisions made will always reflect your inner peace, patience, and desire to do the right thing by all.

———◆———

Freedom from all that wears you down is yours if you choose it.

Know your best self, and you'll know you're doing the right thing.

May 1st

Happiness means different things to different people. It can be found in doing fun things with friends or enjoying a fabulous meal, but what happens when you're alone again? It can be found in doing something you're good at, perhaps sports or hobbies, but what happens when you're not doing it?

A deeper, longer-lasting happiness can be found in finding a sense of purpose in life. When you feel that you're part of something bigger than yourself and that you can make a difference to the lives of others by being who you are and doing what you do, a deeper sense of fulfilment and happiness is found.

True and lasting happiness is always found within. It's in the pursuit of truth, goodness, beauty, and love – fundamental things that may be found in spiritual beliefs or simply in yourself. Happiness is being you as your best self, so look no further than yourself to find it.

The happiness you're looking for is in you.

When you know what matters, you know what doesn't.

May 2ⁿᵈ

Everyone is looking for something in life. Some form a clear vision of what's missing and then set themselves on a path to attaining it, others drift through life with a nagging sense of something being missing but never quite working out what it is.

If you're drifting, you might bounce from one idea to the next, trying without success to fill the void, and finding yourself on a path of repeated disappointments and unhappiness.

Making a conscious effort to get to the heart of what matters most to you in life is the only way to find what's missing. What you're looking for is what brings truth, goodness, beauty, and love into your life; what makes you feel good about being you? Once you know, you have what you need to stop drifting and to be all you can and do all you can to fill your life with meaning and happiness.

———◦◦◦◦———

When something's missing, keep looking for what matters most.

What you seek is what you'll find when you look with purpose.

May 3rd

The journey to becoming all you can be may be long and winding. Discovering which path is the right path for you may take many years or it may take a minute. Much depends on the strength of your conviction and your willingness to be and do better. To become more than you are, you must believe in yourself as more than you are.

To be better and do better, you must believe it's possible to be and do better, and you must then apply your belief to *everything* in your daily life. One grand sweeping gesture is of no value compared to being your best and doing your best in every seemingly mundane thought and action in everyday life.

Only you can hold yourself back from being all you want to be.

The music in your head is the soundtrack to the film playing out in your reality. You can change the music.

May 4th

May the 4th, also known as Star Wars Day to fans of the film franchise, is a day to greet others with, "May the fourth (force) be with you." The force, in this case, is a force for good, giving those who can harness it a means of defeating evil.

It may be a fictional energy in a fictional universe, but in reality, mastery over certain forces within yourself *can* give you the strength and energy you need to control the phenomenal power of your mind.

Every thought is a force that generates an action. If the force is negative, a negative action will follow. When you understand this, you realise that you have the power to change your thoughts, and your thoughts can be a force for good.

———◇◇◇◇◇———

The way you behave is governed by the way you think.

Put your mind to helping others instead of yourself and the deepest peace will be yours.

May 5th

What does it take to be a good person? The simple answer is the giving up of all things that are not good. To be good, you must give up all that is not good – so what is not good?

Selfishness in thoughts or in actions; holding on to ways of thinking and behaving that put your needs ahead of others, and all hollow acts or words of kindness that are only for your benefit and not from the heart. In short, if goodness isn't genuine, it isn't good.

―――――◆―――――

Only through earnest effort can meaningful rewards be earned.

A selfless heart is open to all-comers.

May 6th

It's not possible to become a better you if you're unwilling to make changes for the better. If life is not what you want it to be, then changes need to be made. If you continue to think the same thoughts and behave in the same way, life will continue as it is now: is that what you want? If it's change you want, *you* must change.

In choosing to be a better person, you make the world a better place. In letting go of selfishness, prejudice, anger, hatred, and all unkind thoughts and actions, you make the world around you a much more positive place.

Saying you're making changes for the better does not make you a better person, only *being* better in all you think and do every day, not just when it suits your mood, can change you and your world for the better.

In choosing to treat all with love and compassion, you bring love and compassion into your world.

Thinking bad thoughts can never lead to doing good things.

May 7th

Until you can find it in your heart to treat all others in the same way you wish to be treated yourself, you are no different to everyone else. If you hate those who hate, are you not a hater yourself? If it's okay for you to believe your opinion is more worthy than all others, is it not okay for those others to believe the same of their opinions? If it's okay for you to be angry and impatient with others, why not them with you?

Being a better person is not being better than others, it's being the best you can be in everything you think and do: it's seeing the world beyond yourself and doing the right thing by everyone.

If it's okay for you, it's okay for others. There can be no double standards.

The direct route to selflessness is to give up selfishness.

May 8th

Are you genuine in all you do for others? Are the words you say true to the thoughts in your mind? Are your acts of kindness from the heart, or is there an ulterior motive? Reflecting on these questions and answering them with honesty will give you all you need to know to become a better version of you.

Not everyone you meet will make it easy for you to be your best, but as the Dalai Lama once said, "If you can, help others; if you cannot do that, at least do not harm them."

———◈◈◈◈———

Unless you're willing to learn, there can be no learning.

Let go of all that prevents you from being who you want to be.

May 9th

Time spent thinking about what you don't have and can't do is time spent blinkered to what you have and can do. The focus is negative, so you're only going to see negatives.

Time spent getting angry at the actions of others or thinking badly of others is time spent in a negative frame of mind, leading to others seeing you as the very things you're condemning. Your negativity may be directed at others, but it reflects right back at you.

A truly positive attitude will be clear for all to see in your every thought and every action.

———◈———

Hatred, hostility, and ill will have no place in a right-thinking, right-doing life.

Positivity brings light to even the darkest of days.

May 10th

In a world where "being the best" has come to mean being competitive in everything, both at work and at play, it's no surprise that the true meaning of being your best has become lost. Is it better to win at all costs, or is it better to do your best and play fair?

It's commonly said that "nice guys finish last," but this suggests that only those willing to be selfish, ruthless, and cutthroat will get ahead in life. If this were true, then being the best liar, the best cheat, and the best bully would be considered worthy goals.

Whether you believe yourself to be a spiritual being or not, you *know* in your heart what the true meaning of being your best and doing your best is. It's not riding roughshod over others to get to the front; it's being kind, compassionate, tolerant, and giving. Best is not necessarily first, but being your true best will always make you the true winner in life.

———◈———

Humanity is essentially good.

There is more good than bad in the world.

May 11th

You have everything you need within you to find lasting peace and happiness in your life. Peace and happiness will be found in choosing calm discussion and understanding over heated arguments, choosing love over hate, choosing selflessness over selfishness, and choosing to overcome negativity with positivity. These choices are always yours to make.

———◆◆◇◆◆———

Allow the good in you to see the good in others.

Not all choices bring the outcome you want, but you always have another choice.

May 12th

Knowing what it means to be a good person is of no value if it's not how you live your life. It's not about what you know, it's about what you do. If you know what it is to be kind, but you behave in an unkind way, there's no kindness in your life.

If you know what it is to be selfless, but you think and behave in a selfish way, your actions speak louder than your words. The qualities of being a good person are not something you gain through knowing what they are or being able to recite a list; you only gain them through *being* those qualities in your every thought and action.

———◆———

Goodness and kindness are found in living a good and kind life.

Being good is not a part-time endeavour.

It's not the kindness of others that brings peace into your life, it's *being* kind yourself. The kind thoughts and actions of others can give you a warm and fuzzy feeling, but to fully experience all that kindness can bring into your life, it must be your doing.

Peace is not a mystical experience that only a few will ever experience after years of meditation, it's available to all. Peace is yours to find in yourself when you choose to show genuine kindness in all you think and all you do. Good things are not brought into your life by others, they come to you through your own goodness.

———————◆———————

Be a doer as well as a thinker.

It's only by forgiving that you can experience the joy of forgiveness.

May 14th

If life is lived with a 'what's-in-it-for-me' attitude, there's no room for love in your heart. If your every thought and action is centred on you and what you can gain, there's no love, and there's no peace as you live in fear of losing all you've gained.

Where there's selfishness, there's no room for love. Where there's hate, there's no room for love. Love is found in selflessness, and peace is found in selfless thoughts and acts.

Until you push hatred aside, there's no room for love.

Add love to knowledge and intelligence and you have wisdom.

Real love is unconditional love. Real love comes from within, and it's shown in gentleness, patience, and forgiveness towards all. There are no strings attached. When you can find it in your heart to be kind to others in your every thought and in everything you do, you've found the true meaning of love. In life, the more unconditional love you give, the more love you will receive in return.

Love is only real when it is given unconditionally.

Unless you give freely, you're not giving.

May 16th

When you let go of selfishness, you let go of vanity, pride, greed, and impatience. These things are the source of sorrow and unrest in your life. Choosing to let them go is choosing to create space for happiness and peace to come into your life. A selfless life is a life of love.

———◈———

To be free of frustration, let go of all that frustrates you.

Realise that the thoughts you keep in your mind are the realities you keep in your world.

"Money can't buy me love" is a famous song lyric and, despite the hopes of many lottery ticket buyers, it's also known that money can't buy happiness. It's fair to say that a life without money and the essentials it can buy would be uncomfortable, but true comfort is found in recognising that the luxuries beyond necessities are nothing more than accessories and, as such, can come and go without having any meaningful impact in your life.

To know this is to free yourself from trouble and anxiety. To know this is to understand the value of love, compassion, and kindness over material possessions. With this wisdom, all that is truly meaningful is known, and it's here that peace and happiness is found.

Selfishness is the root of all strife. Love is the root of all happiness.

What's meaningful is known, but it can be hidden under the clutter of what you come to recognise as meaningless.

You need only watch a televised news bulletin to be reminded of the pain and suffering in the world. Witnessing this can leave you feeling helpless. What can one person do to make a difference in a world full of fear and unrest?

In finding inner peace, you're not oblivious to the turmoil faced by others. Inner peace is found in knowing that you are always doing the right thing by yourself and by others. In every thought, you are doing the right thing, and in every action, you are doing what you can to help others.

In being your best and doing your best, you are making a difference in your world. If you can make a positive difference in the life of just one other person, that person can go on to make a difference in the life of another. One person can make a difference.

Ignorance is the root of all so-called evil.

The option of doing the right thing is available now and always.

May 19th

You can't expect to benefit from any changes if you don't actually make those changes. In the same way that you can't expect to see changes in your weight if you don't change your eating habits, or you can't expect to see changes in your fitness if you don't change your exercise habits, you can't expect to see changes for the better in your life if you don't make any changes in the way you currently do things.

Without change, nothing changes. There's no magic wand that can be waved to transform you from who you are to who you want to be, but you can become that person. Change begins the moment you give up the old and embrace the new.

***

Heaven is a place on earth – not just in song lyrics.

Your heaven is in your heart, and it's a place of your making.

May 20th

Nothing is possible until you believe it's possible. To see changes for the better in your life, you must believe those changes are possible. What you choose to believe becomes your reality, so have faith that you can achieve whatever you put your mind to. Know it's true in your heart and your mind, and all you need to achieve it will be yours.

———◆———

All you're looking for will be revealed if you believe it's out there.

Realise that all you need is already yours.

May 21st

To be at peace with the world is to make no demands; to never defend yourself or retaliate; to only do good; to treat everyone with kindness, even those who attempt to hurt you; and to never pass judgement or condemn any other person or belief system. If you can achieve all of this, you will be free from anger, fear, suspicion, jealousy, anxiety, and grief, and you will live a life of love, joy, kindness, and peace.

———◆———

Perfect trust, perfect knowledge, perfect peace; all three are present in a life of selfless love and compassion.

The peace and happiness you're looking for in the world must first be found in your heart.

May 22nd

A strong character is built on strong foundations. The foundation of good character is steadfastness, and the cornerstones are purity, wisdom, compassion, and love. Unless you remain true to these principles in all you think and all you do, the strength of your character will crumble.

Who you are is who you are at heart. There's no steadfastness, purity, wisdom, compassion, or love in presenting a fake façade to the world. If what you say is not what you do, there's no truth in it. There's nothing to be gained from pretending to be something you're not, and everything to be gained from knowing what you truly believe in and building strong foundations to support what truly matters.

———◆◇◆———

Finding all you're looking for takes daily effort and patience in all you think and do.

The price of happiness is abandoning selfishness.

May 23rd

Past and future are dreams; now is reality. You can't change the past and you can't predict the future; you can only act in the present to influence your future. Now, this present moment, is the time to act.

The consequences of *not* acting now are looking back with thoughts of what you might have achieved if you *had* acted, or forever dreaming of a future that you never quite attain.

To act now is to put away thoughts of what might have been or what might never be and to focus on *being* and *doing* in the present moment, because now is reality and now is the only place you can make things happen.

———◆———

Is "not now" code for never?

You have no power over your past. All of your power is in now.

May 24th

If not now, when? Every January, magazines and websites are full of 'New Year, New You' ideas. Everyone thinks they'll start a weight-loss diet in January, or start a new exercise regime, or get a new job, or learn a new skill... the list goes on, but if you haven't been able to do it in May, or September, or any other time of year, what makes January any different?

Whatever it is you want to be, do, or achieve, the time to begin is now. Whatever "new" means to you, you must begin thinking as the new version of you right away and allow those thoughts to power the actions needed to achieve your goal.

———⸪———

Stay on the path... don't stray from it, and don't talk to wolves.

Nike said, "Just do it," but do it now, not later.

May 25th

It's said that the best way to learn something is to teach it to someone else. There are certain things that can be learned from books or from sitting in on lectures, but until you understand those things well enough to be able to teach them to others, you haven't fully absorbed what you're learning. The same can be said of learning a practical skill. Reading about it or watching someone else do it is not the same as doing it yourself.

To be better and do better in life, you need to apply all that you're learning. It's not enough to have knowledge if you're not putting it into daily practice. In being your best in all you do, you're not only honing your skills, you're also showing others what it means to find peace and love in a life of doing the right thing.

———◆———

Be purposeful in all you do, and renew your resolve to be purposeful daily.

Confidence grows through practice, and you grow through confidence.

May 26th

A common piece of advice given to children is, "If you don't have anything nice to say, don't say anything at all." In today's world of passing comment on social media, this sound advice appears to have been forgotten. Idle chit-chat may be seen as harmless conversation, but at what point does conversation become gossip? In treating others as you'd wish to be treated yourself, consider that if it's okay for you to gossip about others, then it's okay for others to gossip about you.

In all conversation, be genuine. If you're changing what you say to fit in with others, you're not being true to yourself. If what you say can't be relied upon, then *you* can't be relied upon. Above all, consider the effect of your words on others. Be truthful in all you say, but be compassionate. Be truthful, but be calm and measured. If you're saying something about someone that you wouldn't say to that someone in person, you *know* that you don't have anything nice to say.

Avoid exaggerations. The true and best version of you is all that's needed.

There's no need to enter into any argument when you're already living the point you're making.

May 27th

As in golf, integrity is key in the game of life. There's no integrity in only doing what you know to be the right thing because others are watching. The rule in golf is that the ball must be played from where it lands. If you thought no one was watching, would you move the ball to give yourself an advantage on your next shot?

Picking and choosing when to do the right thing to suit your own purposes is not doing the right thing. If it matters, it matters *all* the time. Know what matters, stick by what matters, and you will always be doing the right thing.

Self-control and integrity go hand in hand.

There's no childish "he made me do it" in being your best self. There's no finger of blame to point at anyone but yourself.

May 28th

It seems that showing "goodwill toward all men" has become a concept that's only ever remembered around Christmas time, and it's promptly forgotten again as soon as the decorations come down. To show true goodwill, it must be in your every thought and every action all year round.

Goodwill is not just for Christmas. Goodwill is subduing anger and overcoming hatred. It's never being bitter or resentful, choosing instead to meet anger with calmness, mockery with patience, and hatred with love. It's never taking sides, and never disparaging other cultures, beliefs, or religions. It's treating everyone equally, and treating everyone with kindness and compassion. Do all of this, and you are living in the true spirit of goodwill.

In true acts of kindness, all thoughts of self are gone.

In all you do and all you are, be strong, be energetic, and be steadfast.

Sorting fact from fiction can be challenging in a world full of fake news. Falseness is everywhere. From overly sensationalised headlines to photoshopped images, the lines between reality and total fabrication have become blurred.

Knowledge is power, but knowledge must be based on truth. What you hear and what you see can no longer be relied upon as fact, so what you choose to believe must be what you know to be true from your own experience.

Use knowledge and experience to test and understand the theory of cause and effect. Know that thinking good thoughts and selflessly doing good deeds brings lasting happiness and peace into your life, and know that negative thinking can only ever bring more negativity into your life. Know these things and be sure of these things through finding your own truth.

———◈———

Be right-minded, intelligent, and you will always see the truth.

Truth is. There is no chaos in your life. It's only so because you see it as so.

May 30th

The more you know and understand about yourself, the more you grow as a person. The more you recognise the thoughts that help you and those that hinder you, the better placed you are to make meaningful changes for the better.

Understanding yourself helps you to understand others, and in understanding others, you find greater kindness and compassion. To be able to put yourself into the shoes of another is to be able to see beyond yourself. In life, you are moving up a level from selfishness to selflessness.

According to the law of causation, there's no good thought that can create a bad outcome and no bad thought that can create a good outcome.

Make no room for hatred and you have more room for love and understanding.

May 31st

The one person you need to be able to rely on is yourself. No one else can take responsibility for your thoughts and actions. No one can be strong for you unless you are strong for yourself. No one can overcome for you; only you can overcome. No one can learn for you, and no one can put learning into practice for you; only you can do it for yourself.

To be better and do better in life, you must take responsibility for being your best and doing your best in all you think and do. No one else is responsible for the thoughts in your head, the words that come out of your mouth, or the way you behave. Be your best, be true to your best self, and be someone you can trust and rely on.

———◆———

Be self-reliant, but not selfish.

Goodness is the aim of all religions and, irrespective of religious or spiritual beliefs, should be the aim of all.

June 1st

You might think that wealth and status make for a happier life than poverty and hardship, but there's suffering and happiness in life, irrespective of circumstances. For every action, there's a consequence. Rich or poor, your thoughts and actions dictate your outcomes. If you think and behave selfishly and unkindly, you will reap what you sow.

If you think and behave selflessly and with kindness, you will reap what you sow. Just as those with wealth have everything to lose as a consequence of selfish actions, those in poverty have everything to gain as a consequence of selfless actions. Whatever your circumstances, the seeds you choose to sow today determine the harvest you will reap in your tomorrows.

———◆———

Putting yourself before others should never be motivated by anything other than love and compassion.

The painful consequences of selfishness are inescapable.

June 2nd

To switch unhappiness for happiness, a reversal of the thoughts and actions that led to unhappiness is needed. If you know what makes you unhappy, you know what is needed to be happy. In knowing this, you know what you need to change.

Contrary to what many may believe, it's not possible to be happy while thinking and acting selfishly. By the same token, it's not possible to be unhappy while thinking and acting unselfishly. Changing your thoughts and actions can and will bring about change in your life. Happiness or unhappiness is determined by you.

———◆◇◆———

What you determine to be happiness or unhappiness is of your making.

You are limited only by your thoughts.

June 3rd

What you're looking for in life is what you'll find. If your mind is full of suspicious, covetous, envious thoughts, you'll find all you need to confirm those thoughts. In thinking selfish thoughts, you see only selfishness in others, and you'll treat any selfless act you witness with suspicion, convinced of some ulterior motive. In this frame of mind, the world is a mean and miserable place.

Compare this to a mind full of generous, kind, and unsuspecting thoughts. In this frame of mind, the world is a wondrous and beautiful place. In choosing to think positive thoughts, you will find all you need to confirm those thoughts, and you will not only see good things in others, but others will see good things in you, perhaps inspiring a little more positivity in their minds.

The thoughts in your mind determine what you experience in your reality.

Don't let your mind become a harbour for dark and hateful thoughts; allow bright and beautiful thoughts to sail in and brighten your world.

June 4th

You can't know what you don't know, until you know. If all around you share your view of the world, you become unaware of any other view. If all around you behave badly, bad behaviour becomes all you know.

If negativity is the norm in your thoughts, positivity goes unseen. The world inside your head is reflected in your outer environment. Until you open your mind and broaden your view, what you don't know will remain unknown, and all potential to be more than you currently are is lost.

The small-minded and the big-hearted could be neighbours, but they live worlds apart.

Like minds tend to stick together, but to grow, minds need to be stretched beyond what's already known.

June 5th

Your inner thoughts influence your outer reality. Everything that you experience as an event or happening is a combination of your thoughts, your actions, and the actions of others. You can't alter or control the thoughts and behaviours of others, but you can alter your attitude to happenings out of your control.

Instead of trying to mould others into doing things differently, focus your attention on your own thoughts and on what you can do differently to get the most out of any situation.

―――――◆―――――

Things follow thoughts. By altering your thoughts, things can be adjusted.

Your reality is half things and half thoughts.

June 6th

"Sticks and stones may break my bones but names will never hurt me" is an old playground chant that many children learn to help them rise above the taunts of bullies. At any age, the sentiment in these words is a reminder that any hurt that comes your way is not brought by others but by your response to others.

When you know that you are being your best and doing your best in all aspects of life, you are free to rise above all attempts by others to knock you down or hold you back. No one can hurt you unless you choose to be hurt by them. Adopting an attitude of calm understanding rather than reacting or retaliating disarms any effort to cause upset, and the injury becomes the sender's rather than yours as you remain untouched and unfazed.

How others treat you is of no consequence when you rise above it in the way you treat others.

All things outside of yourself are powerless to harm you.

June 7th

Have you ever felt hampered by circumstances? Have you ever complained that if you'd only had this or had that, you could have achieved this or that? If you'd only had money... If you'd only had time... If you'd only had freedom from other commitments... In reality, these things are excuses for not achieving, not valid reasons. All it takes to push through these "hindrances" is a positive 'can do' attitude.

With the right attitude, a way through, over, or around difficulties will always be found, and with the right attitude, those difficulties themselves become stepping-stones that help you learn what you need to know to keep going. With the right attitude, there's no longer any need to find excuses because you're already doing, and through doing, you will achieve.

***

If you're complaining about your circumstances, you're not ready to achieve.

Your attitude is the all-important factor in determining your ability to succeed.

June 8th

In knowing right from wrong, you have a choice. You can knowingly do right, or you can knowingly do wrong. Those who choose wrongdoing may consider themselves freer than right-doers. They can, after all, do whatever they like as they abide by no law, but are they really free? Every action has a consequence.

You might argue that the choices you make are part of your nature, therefore part of who you are, but your nature is your habits, and your habits can be changed. True freedom is found in adapting your nature to be your best, do your best, and always do the right thing.

Good thoughts and good actions are the habits of good people.

There is nothing that can prevent you from accomplishing what you're truly aiming for in life.

June 9th

All that you are is what you have become, and all that you can be is all that you have yet to become. Your character is an accumulation of the repeated thoughts and actions that have become habit, so in effect, your character is your choice.

Repeated patterns of behaviour become so automatic that you're no longer consciously aware of doing them, making it seem that you have no control over them, but just as those patterns became established, new patterns can become established. You are what you think and do, so becoming who you want to be is habitually thinking and acting as the person you are becoming.

———⬦———

Habit is repetition. Fixed habits are what you are.

You can be more than you are by being more in your thoughts.

June 10th

When habits become habits of a lifetime, they may seem impossible to break, but becoming consciously aware of unconscious patterns of behaviour is the first step towards making the break. Habits can be changed.

Old, unhelpful habits can be broken, and new, helpful habits can be established. All it takes is awareness and commitment to making changes for the better.

———◦◦◇◦◦———

You are limited only by your thoughts.

Changing your thoughts changes your habits, your character, and your life.

June 11ᵗʰ

The ancient Greeks believed that to live well, a healthy mind was as important as a healthy body. In modern medicine, the mind-body connection is well recognised, and a troubled mind is closely linked to a troubled body. In the same way that improving your physical health takes time, improving your mental health is not an instant process.

If you want to become physically stronger, faster, or leaner, a progressive programme of exercise is needed, and then it takes effort and commitment to stick with the programme. If you want to become mentally stronger and able to switch from negative to positive thinking, effort and commitment to change is also required.

Change can be uncomfortable, but just as physical effort will bring about physical changes, mental effort will bring about changes in the way you think, which will in turn bring about changes in your whole being.

Your body is the image of your mind.

Harmony in your thoughts is an essential element of whole body wellbeing.

June 12th

In the current system of things, you can't live forever in body, but you can be forever remembered in spirit. If your living days are spent selfishly accumulating material possessions and putting your own needs before others, how will you be remembered? If your life is a constant struggle to get ahead and stay ahead and your days are filled with thoughts of anger, hatred, and frustration, how will you be remembered?

Peace is not something to be found at the end of your days on earth, it is to be found in your living years. Peace is found in selflessness; it's found in compassion and kindness, and it's found in being the best you can be in all you think and all you do.

Being your best is doing the right thing, and doing the right thing is treating others as you'd wish to be treated yourself. The way you choose to live your life will be the way you are remembered.

In considering your immortality, consider how others will remember your life.

Whatever your religious or spiritual beliefs, being remembered with love is at the heart of it all.

June 13th

Death, just as birth, is a part of life as we currently know it. Religious and spiritual beliefs provide different thoughts on life after death, but for many, the belief in eternal spirit is a comforting one. For now, death is a reality for all, and what follows is your legacy.

Choose to live your life thinking good thoughts, doing good deeds, and being your best self, and through your legacy, others will aspire to live their lives in the same spirit of love, kindness, and peace.

———◆———

*A life well lived hopes of becoming a loving memory
to those left behind.*

To leave a legacy of love is the goal of all.

June 14th

If who you are is what you own, what happens if you lose it all? If your worth is based on your physical appearance, what happens when your appearance changes? There's no lasting love in the love of possessions, and there's no lasting peace in vanity.

Who you are is who you are on the inside. With all of your possessions removed and with your looks fading as you age, what's left? Who are you at heart when all else is stripped away? In a selfish frame of mind, this is a tough question to answer. In a selfless frame of mind, the answers you find hold the key to lasting love, peace, and happiness.

———◦◦◦◦———

Wisdom, love, and peace are found in a selfless life.

Seeing love in the world beyond yourself is the realisation of selfless love.

June 15th

Life is change. With age comes physical change. Clinging to youthful pursuits that represent happy times in your mind is a recipe for disaster if your body is unable to keep up. If you're living life in fear of what you're losing, you're missing out on all that you could be gaining.

When you let go of selfish thoughts, a whole new world of happiness becomes available to you. The joy of selflessness has no age limit. As champion boxer Muhammad Ali once said, "The man who views the world at 50 the same way as he did at 20 has wasted 30 years of his life."

Selfishness is asking others to live as one wishes to live.

In life, all external things are transient. What matters most in your heart will always stay with you.

June 16th

Getting caught up in the need for more in a commercialised world is effectively getting stuck in a hamster wheel. There's no end to what you "need" to be happy, and your life will be spent chasing after the next false dream.

Only by stopping and stepping away from the wheel can you begin to see a life beyond it. When you stop running, you give yourself time to reflect on what life is really all about. In looking at life beyond the wheel, you come to realise that the happiness you're chasing will not be found in possessions, it can only be found within you.

Happiness is not what you have, it's what you are; it's in your daily thoughts and actions, and it's in what you can do for others, not what you can accumulate for yourself.

———◆———

There can be no immortality in physical form.

Good is what you do, not what you have.

June 17th

Love knows no bounds. Kindness can be seen everywhere. Inspirational people are found in all walks of life. The wealthy may inspire through philanthropy, the knowledgeable may inspire through teaching, and everyone, everywhere, can inspire through selfless acts and good deeds done.

There's no status or circumstance in life that dictates how you should think and behave; your thoughts and actions are always your responsibility. In choosing to show love and kindness in all you think and do and to treat all as equals, you inspire others to do the same.

———◈———

Compassion for all, not picking and choosing, is true compassion.

What you can do for others should never depend on what they can do for you.

June 18th

The great lesson in life is that true happiness is found in selflessness. Of course, this simple lesson is not so easy to accept and live by when the world is full of messages telling you otherwise. When all around you are selfishly putting themselves before others, should you do the same? In putting others before yourself, are you making yourself a doormat?

Adopting an attitude of "if you can't beat them, join them" may be tempting, but joining them will not bring happiness and peace into your life. Only by being the person you want to be and doing what you know to be the right thing can you bring good things into your life. Be a shining example of true goodness, and others will want to join you.

———◈◈◈———

Only a good deed done selflessly is a good deed. Only a good thought with no thought of personal gain is a good thought.

If all could find goodness in their heart, all would find happiness in life, and all the world would find peace.

June 19th

If all around you is chaotic, how can you find calm? When noise is everywhere, where can quiet be found? If everyday life feels like another day out on the battlefield, is peace ever possible? Calm, quiet, and peace *can* be found, but it requires a conscious step away from the chaos and noise of the "battlefield".

The busyness of life can lead you into thinking that taking time out for yourself would be selfish. In fact, the opposite is true. In thinking that the world around you can't cope without you at the helm for even a short while, you are being selfish. You are not that important.

Selfish is believing that your world will stop if you stop. If this is you, you need to change your thinking. In stepping off the battlefield, you give yourself an opportunity to see your world from a different perspective. In stepping away from the chaos and noise, you give yourself a moment for quiet reflection. In changing your thinking, you may begin to see things as they really are. Is the busyness in your life of your making?

———◆———

The world may be in a constant state of turmoil, change, and unrest, but in maintaining constancy in what matters most, you keep a state of peace and calm in your heart.

To see things as they really are, a childlike view is needed.

June 20th

After war comes peace, but it's never lasting peace. With one side winning and one side losing, there's still hatred. Global peace will only ever be achieved when there's no more hatred and there's a genuine desire for peace in everyone's heart.

On a smaller scale, the same applies to finding peace in yourself. While there's hatred in your heart, you will not find lasting peace. For as long as you choose to pick fights and argue your case, there can be no peace. The peace you find in winning an argument will be short-lived because there will always be another argument to win.

Only when you have a genuine desire to find inner peace will you be able to give up all negativity in your thinking and your actions, and only then will you be able to switch hatred for love, kindness, and compassion.

———◆———

Hatred destroys lives, and through hatred rises persecution and war.

Inner peace can only be found when all hatred is removed from your heart.

Have you ever wished all your troubles would just vanish? Have you ever wished your life could be different? Wishing holds no power, but what you wish for can be yours if you choose to focus your every thought on achieving it. Thoughts have power.

When you choose to conquer yourself, your journey begins. With self-control, you gain wisdom, and with wisdom, you understand that change can't happen unless you make it happen. Change from where you are now to where you want to be requires change in the way you currently think about things and do things.

Unless you're prepared to make those changes and commit to doing whatever it takes for as long as it takes, you're only wishing, and wishes hold no power.

Self-control lights the way to wisdom.

The person you want to be is the real you. Hold this thought in mind, and every thought will guide the actions needed to take you there.

June 22nd

In school, children must learn the basics of a subject before they can progress to a more advanced level. A tutor never attempts to teach complicated mathematical formulae before simple sums have been mastered, and only after mistakes have been made and further learning has taken place can the next level be introduced.

In life as in school, learning must take place one step at a time. It's not possible to know everything there is to know at once, and it's not possible to leap ahead to advanced understanding without fully grasping and applying the basics – and no doubt making a few mistakes.

Lessons in life require the same discipline and practice as lessons in a classroom if you are to learn all you need to know.

Practice precedes knowledge in all things.

June 23rd

A child is taught how to behave through repeated instruction. There's no in-depth detail given to explain why they must behave this way; they're simply conditioned to do as they're instructed. Only after proper behaviour has been established can a child progress to understanding why this is the correct way to behave.

Only by doing can you do the right thing. Only by doing can you learn how to do better. Only by *doing* better can you *be* better, and as you become better, your understanding of what it is to do the right thing grows. By doing, you become.

―――――――――◆◇◆―――――――――

Only by doing can you learn how to do and do well.

Not all you do will be successful, but through failure, you learn how to succeed.

June 24th

Where there's a good heart, goodness lives. Where there's selflessness, goodness lives. Where hate, anger, greed, and pride are banished, goodness lives.

Where goodness lives is not a far-off distant land or a fairy tale kingdom, it's within you. Find love and kindness in your heart; banish selfishness and all negativity, and *you* are where goodness lives.

———◈◈◈———

In learning the lessons that guide you to becoming better, you gain the knowledge you need to become your best.

Clear negativity from your heart and mind, and sweetness will replace strife.

June 25th

To make anything happen, laziness must first be overcome. Laziness may be failing to put full effort into the task at hand, or it may be procrastinating and putting off getting started on the task at all. It may also be shirking responsibility, looking to someone else to make things happen for you, or it may be neglecting the tougher aspects of the task and favouring the easy bits that take less effort.

Until laziness is overcome, nothing can happen. Overcoming laziness becomes easier when every daily task, big or small, is done promptly the moment it arises before any thought of putting it off until later can enter your mind. In this way, the habit of doing is established, and you become a habitual doer rather than a habitual procrastinator.

———◈◈◈———

Never put off until tomorrow what can be done today. Reflect on your day and question whether all you did was all you needed to do.

Make what you need to do what you want to do,
and it will always be done.

June 26th

Success comes to those who have prepared for its arrival. It's rare that opportunity knocks on your door, but if you're waiting for it, you need to be ready to answer. In reality, it's much more likely that those who have found success went looking for it. They didn't sit around waiting for the knock; they went out and did the knocking themselves.

Did opportunity come knocking on the door of the film set sandwich delivery boy who was offered a small part that then launched his acting career, or did he go out knocking on the door himself by getting a job that gave him access to a film set, knowing he wanted to get into acting? Had he not been prepared for the opportunity when it knocked, his bit part would have led to nothing more and he'd still be the sandwich boy. To succeed, you need to be ready for success.

───◈───

Without putting your mind to it, success will remain out of reach.

No effort, no reward.

June 27th

The direct route is always going to be the fastest route – unless there are roadworks. If you come up against a roadblock, do you stop and sit it out, do you turn back, or do you find another way? Unless you choose to find another way, you're not moving forwards. However, if you rush with impatience onto any other available route, you may end up going in the wrong direction. With this being the case, impatience has only led to more delay.

"If at first you don't succeed, try again," is a well-known saying, but it's important to note that if you try again without first giving thought to why you didn't succeed, you will more than likely fail again. If the fastest route to where you want to go is blocked, you do need to find another way, but you also need to take a moment to ensure the way you choose is the best diversion.

In life, getting to where you want to go requires effort, but don't let impatience lead to wasted effort as you become lost on an endless mystery tour.

———◈◆◈———

Anxiety, hurry, and fussiness will not get you to where you want to go any faster than calmness, patience, and acceptance.

Put your energy into learning and improving, not running in circles getting angry and frustrated.

June 28th

Unless you're setting off from the top of a hill, the first few pedal cycles on a bike are going to be the toughest before you can settle into cruising along with much less effort. The same can be said of embarking on any journey of change in life. Getting started is going to take effort, but dedicated effort will lead to progress, and the effort will become lighter as new habits become established.

This might be considered a cruising along stage, but if you want to make further progress, further effort will once again be required. In life, as on a cycle ride, getting to new places will always require renewed effort. How far you go will be determined by how much effort you're prepared to put in.

———◈———

Enduring success comes to those who calmly and steadily progress more than those who try to hurry progress along.

The root of success is in character, and your habits are your character.

June 29th

You can learn from failure, but you can also learn from success.
Failure is not a prerequisite to success, but accepting that failure *is*
an option is key to getting past the fear of failure that holds so
many back. Through success, you learn what works, and through
failure, you learn what doesn't work. Where fear takes hold is
where there's an unknown.

Where things haven't gone to plan and failure has been experienced
and moved on from, thoughts of, "What if this doesn't work; what if
this all goes wrong?" are replaced with, "What if this *does* work, only
one way to find out." Where failure has yet to be experienced,
the "what ifs" remain negative.

Failure remains an unknown, and fear of failure can become
paralysing. When you understand this, you realise that failure can lead
to greater progress overall than success, and while success can build
confidence, experiencing failure and learning how to move on from it
builds even greater confidence.

Both success and failure teach valuable lessons.

*Success and failure are part of life. If life became constant failure,
all confidence would be lost, but constant success can also create a
fear of failure that strips all confidence to achieve more away.*

June 30th

When things don't go to plan, it's not because those things conspired against you. When you're running late, and every traffic light is at red, it's not the traffic lights conspiring against you that makes you late, it's you not leaving early enough. When you're not paying attention and you burn the meal you have in the oven, it's not because the oven conspired against you, it's because you forgot to watch the time.

Wanting all things to accommodate your particular needs is wanting the universe to bend to your will. Things are as they are and have no need to be anything other than they are. All things are perfect; the only imperfection is your attitude.

Rather than rage at the world and expect all to go your way, calmly change your attitude and adjust your thoughts and actions to see things as they really are.

Things are as they are and can't be moulded to your will.

If all you see around you is imperfection, you must recognise it in yourself.

July 1st

Where you are now does not determine where you can go next. Your circumstances are not you, and only you can decide what limits you put on yourself. Comparing yourself and what you have to someone else and what they have is of no value.

What is of value is comparing who you are now to who you want to be. What needs to change to move from one into the other? You already have all you need within you; you just need to recognise the thoughts and actions that are helping you to move and those that are keeping you stuck.

You are stuck if you think you're too poor. It's not wealth that gives you what you need to be your best and do your best in all you do. You are stuck if you think you've had too many upsets and setbacks.

Will adding more negativity to the mix resolve those upsets? There's nothing that can't be overcome if you choose to find a way. The limits you put on yourself are the only thing keeping you stuck where you are.

Wisdom is the aim of every philosophy.

Are you going to cry over spilt milk, or are you going to mop it up and carry on?

July 2nd

Overcoming another with force is a show of strength, but self-control, and thereby overcoming yourself, is a show of might. Becoming the master of someone else by using force is only a win until someone else comes along and uses force to win against you. There's no lasting peace. When you learn how to master yourself, you win.

Self-control is true power. With self-control, you are no longer a slave to changing emotions or to temptations. With self-control, you never lose sight of what matters most, and with self-control, you can rely on yourself to always do the right thing. With self-control, you have lasting peace.

———◆◇◆———

Self-control is mightier than force.

There's no mightier power than having control over yourself.

July 3rd

When you know what truly matters to you, and you know that those things bring lasting peace and happiness into your world, there's nothing that can tempt you away from them. Others may continue to search for happiness in material things and continue to be slaves to ever-changing fashions and trends, but you already have all you need.

Self-control gives you all you need to remain true to yourself. There's no need to follow the crowd when you already know that what others are searching for can only be found in themselves, not in external things.

Others may hate, but you can choose love; others may condemn, but you can choose forgiveness; others may cling to possessions, but you can let go; and others may continue to blindly join the bandwagon, but you can see things as they really are.

With self-control comes wisdom and the ability to see things as they really are.

When you have all you need internally, there's no need to search externally.

July 4th

In choosing to live life as your best self, you become invincible. When you have integrity, you have nothing to hide. When you tell no lies, there's no tangled web to get caught in. When you have no secrets, there are no skeletons in the closet.

When you are genuine in all you think and do, you are deceiving no one. As your best self, you have no thoughts or actions to be ashamed of, so any words or acts of hatred, slander, or envy that come your way can have no effect – the only shame is on those choosing to live a life full of anger and hatred.

Harm no one, and there's no one to fear.

Choose to live right and you can't be wronged.

July 5th

To "love thy fellow man" is not to agree with or go along with all others say and do, it's to be tolerant and understanding of others and to choose kindness and compassion over hate and condemnation.

When there's no hate in your heart, the hate of others has no power over you. When there's only kindness and compassion in your heart, the unkindness of others has no power over you. The power of love will always overcome all.

Love conquers all.

Love is the only lasting power.

July 6th

Love is not just seen in what you do, it's who you are. When the spirit of love guides your every thought and action, you have the knowledge and power you need to find your way through every difficulty.

The way to love is self-mastery. Knowing who you are and what matters most to you gives you the power to live your life in a meaningful way, secure in the knowledge that you are thinking the right things and doing the right things.

With the spirit of love, you are your own master, and in choosing to do no harm to any other, there's no harm that can come to you. In the spirit of love, just as in the spirit of all classic comic books, good will always overcome evil.

———◆———

To do no harm in thoughts or actions is to know love.

With love in your heart, you have nothing to fear.

July 7th

In selfishness, fear of missing out or fear of not having the latest 'must have' items keeps you in chains, forever enslaved to selfish wants and desires. In selflessness, freedom is found.

Freedom is found in knowing what it means to be and do your best, and in knowing what matters most. In selfishness, you will always want more; in selflessness, you already have all you need.

Freedom is found in realising that happiness is not found in things; it's found in you. It's not what you have and what others can do for you; it's who you are and what you can do for others.

———◈———

In becoming your best self, you find freedom.

Knowing what matters sets you free from all that doesn't matter.

July 8th

Eleanor Roosevelt once said, "No one can make you feel inferior without your consent." These are wise words. If you're feeling that you're not good enough, where is that feeling coming from? You might think it's coming from the way someone else has spoken to you or behaved around you, but this is not the case. It's coming from your own mind.

There's nothing anyone else can say or do to make you feel inferior unless you believe yourself to be inferior in your own thoughts. What you think impacts the way you feel, and the way you feel influences everything you experience as your reality.

By changing your thoughts, you can change the way you feel. If you feel good enough, you *are* good enough. If you feel you're not good enough, you're not. When you understand this, you realise that the words and actions of others have no control over you or how you feel. The control is yours.

To find freedom, you must free yourself.

What you choose to believe is what you will experience.

Should you aim for goodness or for greatness? After all, to have high aspirations is to achieve great things, so why not aspire to greatness? The problem here is that without goodness, there can be no greatness. If you're aiming for greatness, your motives are selfish. In wanting to be great, you're looking for recognition, admiration, and personal gain.

If, however, you're aiming for goodness, your motives are entirely selfless. In wanting to be good, you have no need for recognition or admiration; you simply want to be kind, compassionate, and caring in your every thought and in all you do for others. There is no thought of personal gain.

Those aiming for greatness will fail, but those aiming for goodness may achieve unsolicited greatness in the hearts and minds of others through all they selflessly do.

———◈◇◈———

Be childlike in your view of the world and you will always see the beauty, not the beast.

Your greatness will always be found in your goodness.

July 10th

Many a child has heard a parent say, "Do as I say, not as I do." On many levels, these words make no sense at all. In the same way that a duckling instinctively follows a mother duck's lead and does as she does, a child will instinctively do the same.

What a parent *says* will always take a backseat to what they *do*. As a parent, if you know that what you're doing is not what you want your child to do, you need to ask yourself why you're doing it. If you know it's not a good thing to do, why are you doing it?

If what you say is not what you do, your words have no power to influence. It's what you do that influences. In thinking good thoughts, doing good deeds, and being your best, as well as doing your best in all you do, your actions are inspiring the thoughts and actions of all around you.

Through living life as your best self, you positively influence the lives of all who see the benefits, and your influence is then passed on through all who do as you do.

To be good is to promote all that's good.

In always being your best, you teach others by example.

July 11th

Imagine thoughts as seeds being planted into the soil of the mind. They develop and grow until they blossom into deeds, and those deeds may be good or bad, brilliant or stupid, depending on the nature of the seeds. After blossoming, they then become seeds of thought again, this time in the minds of others.

Using this analogy, someone sowing seeds into the minds of others is a teacher, but if you are someone teaching yourself through your own experiences, you are a wise farmer.

Just as time is required for a planted crop to fully develop and grow, so it is with thoughts. It takes time for each planted thought to fully develop into knowledge and then blossom into wisdom.

———◆———

Thoughts are seeds that germinate into more of the same.

The seen is the mirror of the unseen.

Anything worth achieving is going to require effort. If you're not prepared to put the necessary work in, you're not going to get the outcome you want. If it's change you want, there's no right time to begin or perfect moment to wait for; the effort must begin the moment the decision to change is made.

Effort requires energy, but in putting all the energy you have into the task in hand, the more energy you create in return, allowing you to keep working towards your goal. If the effort you put in is half-hearted, the energy return will diminish accordingly, and your goal will remain in the distance.

Unfocused energy is wasted energy.

Full effort is focused effort. Unnecessary noise and hurry are nothing more than wasted energy.

July 13th

Where there is calmness in effort, there is the greatest power.
Calmness indicates a strong, well-trained, patient, and disciplined
mind. Calm workers know their business. They may have little to say,
but what they do say matters.

Everything they do is well planned, and seeing ahead to the end
point, they make straight for it with no fuss, no delay, and no wasted
energy. They have prepared for all eventualities and are therefore
never taken by surprise. Never in a hurry, they are sure of their
abilities and calmly confident in all they do.

———⊰⊱———

It is a great delusion that more noise means more power.

*Where there's unnecessary noise, there's wasted effort. The person
complaining the most is the person achieving the least.*

Calmness should not be confused with being laidback. Laidback suggests easy-going, but calmness differs in that it's focused and concentrated energy. The energy of an excitable, fussy person can be wasted in fits of agitation and frustration as they hurry the task in hand.

The concentrated energy of calmness is much more deliberate. This not only allows the task to be completed skilfully, it means more can be achieved without any need for hurry. The controlled energy of calmness generates success, whereas the excitable energy of hurriedness is simply wasted with no gain.

To move requires energy. To keep moving, no energy must be wasted.

Without the energy to do it, it can't be achieved.

Every success story must have a beginning. In every tale of rags-to-riches, the starting point is rock bottom. It's a safe place to begin as the only way is up, but not wanting to be seen there can lead many to pretend their circumstances are different. In pretending to be wealthier than they are, they spend beyond their means in the mistaken belief that a certain lifestyle is necessary to climb the ladder of success. The outcome is the return to rock bottom.

Success is not the trappings that come with it. Whatever it is you want to succeed in, being true to yourself, irrespective of current circumstances, is key to achieving it. Starting from where you are and being authentic in all you do will allow you to climb steadily towards your goal. Exaggeration and extravagance may lead to a crashing fall. Who you are is success, not what you have.

The spendthrift can never become rich, but if they happened to start out rich, they would soon end up poor.

The thrifty and prudent are on the way to riches.

July 16th

Time and money spent on creating an image is vanity at best and fakery at worst. The trend for film and music stars to "reinvent" themselves has created a false belief that all it takes to become someone different is a change of style, whether it's clothing, hair, or cosmetic surgery.

If you want to be a different person from the one you are now, changing your appearance on the outside does nothing to change who you are on the inside. Changing the way you look can't change the way you feel, and the way you feel is who you are.

True change comes from within; it comes from changing your thoughts, the way you feel, and the way you behave. If you feel ugly, pretty clothes won't change that. For as long as you believe yourself to be ugly, you will continue to think and behave the same way – your clothes change nothing.

If you feel you're not good enough, dressing in the way those you admire dress does not change the way you see yourself. True change must come from the inside out; it can't be done from the outside in.

———◦◇◦———

Vanity is a vice, not a virtue.

Dressing to impress has no effect if in your thoughts you're unimpressed with yourself.

July 17th

"The early bird catches the worm" is just one of many expressions that allude to the need to get up and at it if you want to get ahead in life: "Early to bed and early to rise, makes a man healthy, wealthy, and wise" is another.

While it's true that many successful people throughout history have been early risers (Thomas Edison and Winston Churchill, to name just two), it's not so much the time you get up that makes the difference, it's the attitude in which you start your day. Getting up with a plan for the day ahead makes it much less likely that you'll drift into your day and lose half of it before you've put your mind to anything productive.

A focused mind is a much more productive mind, so it's not the hour on the clock that matters, it's the time you're giving yourself to be up and ready to get the most out of the day ahead, instead of rolling out of bed at the last minute.

Money wasted can be restored; health wasted can be restored; but time wasted can never be restored.

Skill is gained with an attentive attitude.

July 18th

Skill is acquired through diligent practice, and learning the right way to do something will involve the experience of doing it the wrong way – often many times. Efficiency in a skill is getting it right without getting it wrong quite so many times.

Efficient people learn from their mistakes and take what they learn forwards with them. The understanding they gain from each failure is used to limit the potential for failure next time, and in being open to learning in this way, they quickly become much more efficient in all they do.

Learning from the experiences of others will also help you to learn the right way of doing something without having to go through all the wrong ways to get there. However, just like learning from your own mistakes, you need to be open to learning if you are to learn anything.

Unless you're open to finding a better way, you won't find it. If you always think that you know best or that your way is the best way, you're limiting your potential to become much more efficient in all you do.

Wisdom is the highest form of skill.

Efficiency is doing, but doing it better.

July 19th

Any gains made by a fraudster can only ever be short-lived. Crimes will eventually need to be paid for, and it can be a heavy price to pay. The same can be said of anyone trying to get something for nothing in life, not just money. There can be no genuine gains if no genuine effort has gone into acquiring them.

Whatever it is you want, unless *you* are willing to put in the effort required to achieve it, you're no different to a swindler, and your ill-gotten gains will never be yours to keep.

————◆◆◆————

There's no effortless way to achieve what you want.

There's no true prosperity if it's not paid for with moral and intelligent effort.

July 20th

Integrity is doing the right thing, even when no one is looking. Thinking that it's okay not to do the right thing "just this once" is flawed thinking as acting without integrity in just one area of life renders you without integrity across all areas.

In sport, many elite athletes have said that to succeed, you have to "keep working when no one is watching." In life, as in sport, it's the level of work you continue to put in when no one is watching that determines your success.

Genuine integrity is seen in your every action, even when it's unseen by anyone but you.

Integrity must be an integral part of you.

July 21st

It's often said, but honesty really is the best policy. Without honesty, integrity is lost. Without honesty, authenticity is lost. And without honesty, your conscience can never be clear. Bending the truth once generally leads to bending the truth a second time when a further lie is needed to back up the first.

There can be times when "a little white lie" is told with a clear conscience because it was told with the interests of someone else at heart, but every lie told with your own interests at heart is a permanent blot on your character. Dishonesty leads to guilt that can last a lifetime, even if you're never caught in your lies.

Dishonesty is a shortcut to nowhere.

In the bigger picture, there's no escape from dishonesty.

July 22nd

Honesty and integrity are lofty moral principles, but they are only of value if they are put into practice in daily life. Honesty *most* of the time is not honesty, and integrity most of the time is not integrity.

In knowing that you are always doing the right thing, peace is found, so true peace of mind can only come from knowing that you are *always* being your best and doing your best. In knowingly being or doing less than your best, your lofty moral principles become meaningless.

Strength is found in purpose, and in purpose is found achievement.

Morals only have meaning if you live by them.

July 23rd

To join a protest march or to noisily campaign against the unfair working conditions endured by poverty-stricken employees in sweatshops is *not* being sympathetic to a cause if you are buying and wearing clothes manufactured in those sweatshops: it's being a hypocrite.

Campaigning against cruelty to animals is not championing a worthy cause if you then beat your disobedient dog: it's hypocrisy. There is no sympathy in your mind or heart if what you claim to care deeply about is not what you show in your every thought and every action in everyday life.

───◈───

The test is in how you act in the moment, not in your sentiments after the moment has passed.

Sympathy is a deep level of caring within you, revealed in consistent selflessness and consideration for others.

July 24th

True sympathy comes from a place of understanding or of shared experience. You may not have been in their shoes, but you can sympathise with another through having experienced the mental or physical challenges they face in some other way. These experiences bring genuine sympathy for others into your heart.

You can never be involved in the humiliation of another when you know what it is to be humiliated yourself. You can never pass cruel or thoughtless judgements upon others when you know how it feels to be unfairly judged yourself. If you are to be truly sympathetic, there can be no place for thoughtlessness, conceitedness, or selfishness in your heart.

———◦❖◦———

Lack of sympathy is revealed in egotism; sympathy in love.

In its real and profound sense, sympathy arises from shared experiences of suffering.

July 25th

To bring all that is good into your life, be giving in all you think,
say, and do. Be generous in your thoughts as well as your actions,
be giving of your time, be trusting of others, show forgiveness, and be
cheerful in all you do. Do these things willingly, and all will be
returned to you.

———◆◇◆———

Just as cleanliness is next to godliness, so too is gentleness.

Gentleness is wisdom in kindness.

July 26th

In gentleness, wisdom is found. Where there's gentleness, there's no need for quarrels or for angry retaliation when harsh words are spoken. Instead, there's calm composure and a gentle word, together more powerful than any outburst of rage.

The wisdom of gentleness comes from having learned how to control your own anger, giving you the understanding you need to overcome it in others. When you have it, you're saved from the turmoil of uncontrolled emotions and the draining effects of getting caught up in heated battles of will and wars of words. With gentleness, you have all the strength you need to quietly win all of life's battles.

———⊱⋅☩⋅⊰———

Gentleness prompted by thoughtfulness and kindliness will always find friends.

Arguments only reach skin deep; sympathy reaches all the way to the heart.

July 27th

In trying to appear as something you're not, the only person you fool is yourself. There's no harm in the "fake it till you make it" school of thought when all you're doing is stepping into the mindset of the person you're working on becoming and actively making changes for the better in all you think and do.

But when you're being fake and putting no real or genuine effort into making those changes, it's no longer harmless. You're now just a fake, and you won't make it. Faking it with no intention of changing anything about the real you is simply putting on a disguise; you're a sham. The more disguises you wear, and the more about you that's false, the more you lose all identity – you become no one.

Spurious things have no value. Counterfeit is deceit, whether it's people or things.

On authenticity, credibility and reputation are built.

July 28th

In becoming a better you, you free yourself from all your old doubts, fears, hates, dislikes, and every other negative emotion that dragged you down and held you back, and you step into the freedom of a life full of calmness, patience, happiness, and peace.

As the old is left behind, you move into the new, and all the new experiences of good give you everything you need to keep moving forwards without ever looking back.

———◆———

Negativity is an experience, not an unbreakable power.

Wrongdoing is a state of ignorance, and as such it can be made to disappear when the light of knowledge is shone upon it.

July 29th

To have achieved the highest level of virtue in your life and be living those virtues in all you do and in all you are is to enjoy the highest level of blissful happiness. In religious or spiritual beliefs, this highest level may be heavenly, divine, or otherworldly, but whatever your beliefs, in achieving this level, there can be no more unhappiness.

Where unhappiness still exists, it will be where virtues are mingled with lingering thoughts and acts of selfishness. When you become willingly selfless in all you do and in all you are, blissful happiness will be yours.

———◦≈◇≈◦———

Where the highest level of good is practised, life is bliss.

Happiness lies upward and beyond.

You can't pray for peace and yet continue to get into every argument going. You can't despise others without being despised yourself. You can't oppose the ideas of others without others opposing yours. For as long as you have conflict in your heart, you can't have peace, and for as long as you have hatred in your heart, you're shutting love out.

———◆◇◆———

Where there's passion, there's no peace; where there's peace, there's no passion.

By way of learning self-control, perfect peace is achieved.

July 31st

Imagine a world in which everyone understands that you can't stamp out violence with violence. Imagine if everyone understood that their wrongdoing can't undo the wrongdoing of someone else.

If you retaliate with hate, the hate in the world increases. If you find love in your heart, there's a little less hate in the world. If everyone understood this, and understood that where there's hate, there will always be sorrow, would they cease to hate?

If everyone understood that every hateful thought is a seed that grows into a crop of hate, a crop that feeds all around them, would they choose to plant different seeds? Not everyone understands, but you do. The seeds you sow will become the crop you harvest in your world, and the crop that feeds all around you.

———◦◦◦◦———

If only all could understand that being wronged can never be resolved by doing wrong.

If only all could understand that love conquers all.

August 1st

Where you find gentleness, patience, humbleness, graciousness, selflessness, and self-control, you find wisdom. With this wisdom comes insight, and all that's real and true can be distinguished from all that's fake and meaningless. If you find these traits in someone, spend time with them, and let their positive energy influence your every thought and action.

Abandon self, and you can overcome all.

To centre your life around love is to enter into rest, harmony, and peace.

August 2nd

Ditching an unhelpful habit is good, but if you're continually fighting the temptation to pick it up again, this is not so good. There's no peace until all the fighting has stopped. If you've quit smoking, but your thoughts are full of all you miss about smoking, you're not enjoying all that you've gained.

Until your focus is switched from what you don't have to what you have, the fighting continues. The ceasefire begins when you choose to focus on positives, and peace becomes permanent when you choose to keep looking ahead, never back.

There's no peace if you're fighting temptation.

Focus on what you have, and maintain a positive outlook.

No one ever lies on their deathbed wishing they'd spent more time at the office. These words are often said as a reminder that life has a way of twisting what's important and what's not, and it's often not until time is running out that it's realised.

Is what you believe to be important *really* important? Is the way you're living your life the legacy you want to leave behind after you're gone? Life isn't all fun and games, but taking time to reflect on what really matters most *now* will help you to live your life as the person you want to be.

If you're failing to see that being your best and doing your best extends beyond just you, you may have some twisted priorities that need to be straightened out.

Becoming your best is always doing your best.

Live each moment as a legacy.

August 4th

Happiness is... If asked to give three endings to complete this sentence, what would they be? Would they be materialistic things, items that you've always hankered after; would they be delicious foods or drinks that bring you instant pleasure, or would they be what you believe you *should* say – perhaps world peace, an end to all hunger, and a cure for all diseases?

With these last three choices, you might think you're demonstrating selflessness, but nothing could be further from the truth. A selfless act is not a selfless act if it's done to *appear* selfless. If what you're doing is done to impress others, it's not selfless, it's selfish.

Lasting happiness *is* found in selflessness, but to find it, you need to strip away all external influences. Happiness is found in knowing what really matters to *you* and in what you really want in your life, so it will never be found if you're looking in the wrong places.

If you're searching for it in what you believe you *should* want, you're not going to find it, and until what you want is something you're genuinely prepared to commit to achieving, you won't achieve it.

———◆◇◆———

Self and error are synonymous.

What makes you genuinely happy is what really matters.

August 5th

How many of the difficulties you have in your life are of your own making? How many of the problems you have today will you look back on a couple of months or a year from now and wonder why you ever thought of them as problems? When you let go of all selfish thoughts, desires, opinions, and prejudices, you let go of so many difficulties of your own making. If it's all about you, then every time something doesn't go your way, there's going to be upset for you.

Imagine if you could feel genuinely happy for the winner, even when you're the loser; imagine if you could be genuinely happy for others without feeling any thoughts of envy; imagine if you could feel genuinely content just being who you are and doing what you do without feeling the need to keep up with the latest trends, have all the latest gadgetry, or have an image that must be maintained.

What if you could say, "It doesn't matter," and genuinely mean it. Imagine it, and think about the peace it would bring into your life. How many of the difficulties you imagine you have in your life would vanish instantly if you gave up all selfish thoughts?

———◆———

The difficulty with difficulties is letting them go.

In seeing beyond yourself, you see solutions to difficulties.

August 6th

When you know what truly matters to you, you have what you need
to overcome all challenges that come your way. Life is unpredictable
and unexpected happenings can be overwhelming, but when you
have true values and principles that you can stand by, you have
all the support you need in troubled times.

Until your values are your own, you don't have that rock-solid support.
True values remain with you, no matter what. Adopting the beliefs
and values of others may suit certain circumstances, but if they're not
your own, they're subject to change, and change brings uncertainty.

With your own rock-solid values in place, no matter how
unpredictable life can be, you can be certain that you have
all you need to do the right thing.

There is no value in values that are not your own.

Failing to stand by your values is letting yourself down.

August 7th

How do you argue against arguments? You can't. If you're choosing to argue your point, then your point is lost. How do you push forward the need for patience? You can't. If you're pushing, you're being impatient. To make the case for patience, you need to demonstrate patience. To prove the pointlessness of arguments, you need to demonstrate a different and better way.

It's easy to be calm and patient when all around you is calm, but the real test comes when the pressure is on. It's easy to be kind and considerate when others are being kind and considerate around you, but the real test comes when you're faced with unkindness and a lack of consideration.

Patience is only a virtue if you are patient under *all* circumstances. Kindness is only a virtue if you're kind under *all* circumstances. True virtues are not something you need to prove to be true to anyone other than yourself. When they are simply who you are, always, and the way you choose to live your life, always, the truth is clear for all to see.

———⬦———

True patience and forgiveness remain true under all circumstances.

The truth will always out: be true to yourself.

August 8th

When you come to realise what truly matters to you in life and what doing the right thing means to you, you find lasting peace. When you know in your heart what it means to be your best and do your best in your every thought and every act, you never again face an agonising dilemma.

Doing the right thing is what you do; it's not a decision you agonise over. Being your best self is not something you need to give thought to; it's who you are and what you do without any conscious effort, no matter what.

———◈———

To understand and adopt the power of love is to become immortal, invincible, indestructible.

True love is everlasting.

August 9th

When all selfishness is given up, you give without any thought of receiving, and you always give your best, never looking for reward. In the same way that a farmer can do no more than his best in planting the seeds and then put his trust in the elements to bring about a crop to harvest, you can do nothing more than your best as you sow the seeds of goodness, love, and peace.

There can be no expectation in your work; you put your trust in the seeds you sow bringing about a crop of their own kind in due course.

Truth cannot be limited.

Through self-sacrifice and perseverance, you will become all you can be.

All the wisdom of the past points to selflessness as the way to inner peace and happiness. Wisdom is not found in reading and learning about the way to find it; it can only be found in practising what you know and understand to be the way to find it. The path to wisdom can only take you there if you choose to follow it.

Looking for different paths, easier paths, shorter paths, or paths that justify your choice to stray from the original path are all diversions that will delay your journey and may even lead you in the wrong direction. Wisdom is not just what you know, it's what you do, and therefore wisdom should never be confused with intellect.

———◆———

Through restraint, you free up energy to be and do better.

"The only true wisdom is in knowing you know nothing" – Socrates

August 11th

All of your sorrows, your anxieties, and your fears are your own. You can cling to them, or you can let them go. Either way, it's your choice, no one else's. No one else can make you cling; no one else can make you let go. No one else can cling for you; no one else can let go for you. These choices are yours to make, and any changes you want to make can only ever be made by you.

———◇———

Only when you recognise your true self can you be said to be in your right mind.

Give up all selfish thoughts and peace will be yours.

August 12th

If you have reached a place of peace and happiness in your every thought and every action, then you have reached a place from where you can teach others. In this place, there's never any doubt in your mind, there's no sorrow in your heart, and never any despair. In this place you harbour no opinions or false beliefs, not even for a moment; there's no hate or prejudice, no anger or envy, only gentleness, forgiveness, and love.

Until all of this is unconditionally true, you have not reached this place, and therefore it's not your place to teach others. Only by finding and *living* your own peace and happiness can you show others how to find it in themselves.

***

Choose to come out of the storms of wrongdoing and anguish.

Enter the tranquillity of your inner resting place.

August 13th

Never ask someone else to do something that you wouldn't do yourself. Never speak to someone in a way other than you would wish to be spoken to yourself. Never create one rule for you and another for other people, and always put yourself in the shoes of another, choosing empathy over condemnation.

Do these things and you are following the Golden Rule of doing unto others as you would have them do to you, and in putting the happiness of others before your own, you will receive untold happiness in return.

———◈◈◈———

Make yourself sincere and lovable, and you will be loved by all.

Be friendly towards others and others will be friendly towards you.

August 14th

The phenomenal power of the mind is a scientific fact. In sports psychology, it's a well-established fact that mental skill is every bit as important as physical skill if a top performance is to be realised.

In education, it's now recognised that a child's ability to reach their true potential lies in the development of a growth mindset, not just academic ability, and in all other areas of life, the importance of maintaining good mental health as well as physical health is firmly established.

Your physical health is hugely influenced by your mental health. Negativity in your mind has a negative impact on your body, and positivity a positive impact. To be your best and do your best, consider the thoughts in your head and pay attention to the very real effect they have on your actions.

In thinking good thoughts, you create an aura of goodness around you that positively impacts all who enter it.

The root of all negativity and wrongdoing is in the mind.

August 15th

While there's anger, worry, jealousy, greed, or any other negative emotion in your mind, there's going to be a corresponding element of negative physical health in your body. You reap what you sow, and negative thoughts are effectively diseased seeds.

In improving your thoughts, you give your whole body a lift. For as long as selfishness, hatred, suspicion, and all other niggling sources of misery are coursing through your veins – so to speak – there will be niggling physical ailments that accompany them.

Let good thoughts, loving thoughts, and joyful thoughts flow through you, and you're giving your body all the medicine it needs.

⟡

Renounce negativity; welcome positivity.

Live without friction and you smooth your journey through life.

August 16th

If you imagine your journey through life as a voyage across a great ocean, keep the seas calm by keeping control of your emotions. Anger, jealousy, hatred, prejudice, and all forms of negativity will create huge waves in turbulent waters that will threaten to sink your ship.

Instead, keep positivity at the wheel and have faith in your ability to navigate every storm, returning quickly to calm waters and plain sailing through kindness, compassion, and love.

———◆———

Order your thoughts and you order your life.

Let positivity guide you under all circumstances.

Without purpose, there's potential to drift. When your heart is not in what you're doing, there's a tendency to give it less than your best. If you're drifting through life, wishing for something better, there's a very real possibility that you'll miss the opportunity you've been waiting for when it arises.

You get out of life what you put in, so if you're putting in less than your best, opportunities are not going to be queuing up to knock on your door. In failing to give *all* you're doing your best effort, no matter how menial the task, you're failing to keep yourself ready and prepared to move up the ladder when an opportunity presents – or even see the opportunity at all.

As someone wise once said, "Opportunity is missed by most because it comes dressed in overalls and looks like work."

Be big-hearted, loving, and unselfish, and your influence and success will be lasting.

Intention plus concentrated effort equals accomplishment.

August 18th

There will be times in life when others, seeing you fail and coming up against countless setbacks, will tell you to give up on your goal and choose a different, less challenging path.

There may be times when those around you try to persuade you against even setting out on a certain path in the first place, telling you that "it's not for the likes of you" or that you have ideas above your station in life. Such negativity can lead to questioning yourself and perhaps giving in to those unsupportive opinions.

To succeed on any path in life, you need to believe in your ability to succeed. Self-belief is a mental skill, and like any other skill, it can be learned, practised, and mastered. With self-belief, you have the power to find a way through setbacks and difficulties, and most importantly, you have the resilience to stick by what you know to be true.

———◆———

*Passion is not power, it is the abuse of power,
and the dispersion of power.*

Be of single aim and devote yourself unreservedly to achieving it.

August 19th

Whatever your version or interpretation of heaven and hell on earth may be, they are both places that exist within you, and they are both of your own making. When your version of heaven on earth is found in satisfying every selfish need, there's always going to be the need for more.

If heaven on earth is found in a slice of decadent cake or in the buying of a luxurious item, the satisfaction is short-lived, and the desire for more soon returns. In this sense, your version of heaven on earth is in fact your hell on earth – you can never escape the need for more to find happiness.

Lasting happiness can only be found when it comes from within, so true happiness will only be found when heaven on earth is found in selflessness.

———◈———

Happiness is an inward state of satisfaction, joy, and peace.

Heaven and hell on earth are inward states.

August 20th

For as long as you sink into selfishness, you sink into a hell on earth. Only when you choose to rise above it, can you find a heaven on earth. If you are selfishly seeking your own happiness, it will elude you. Only by selflessly putting the happiness of others before your own will happiness come to you.

Seeking selfish wants will only lead to losing happiness.

Give up selfishness, and happiness will come to you.

August 21st

If there's an imaginary ladder that takes you from pain to peace, putting the needs of others before your own is a necessary step to elevate yourself from where you are onto the first rung. For as long as you cling to selfishness, where you are is where you'll stay.

The first rung is only a step away, and your climb away from pain can begin the moment you choose to take that step.

———◆———

What you reflect and meditate on, you will come to understand, and you will grow into its likeness.

If you dwell on selfish and valueless thoughts, you will ultimately become selfish and valueless.

August 22ⁿᵈ

Make it a routine part of your day to spend time in quiet reflection or meditation. Just as brushing your teeth is a daily routine that you always make time for, do the same for quiet time.

There's no right or wrong time, but early in the morning can be a good starting point as the stresses and excitements of the previous day will have been rested away and there's renewed energy available to help you make the start of each new day a good one.

———◆———

Through meditation, you enter into profound and abiding peace.

The lazy and self-indulgent will never know what it is to be and do better.

August 23rd

If you are prone to anger, hatred, or flights of temper, quiet time in reflection should be spent becoming aware of the thoughts and behaviours that accompany these emotions.

Once aware, efforts can be made to change these thoughts and emotions to gentleness and forgiveness, and in time, hatred will make way for love to come into your heart.

Only in quiet reflection, away from external influences and distractions, can you take a good and honest look at where you could do better and be better in everyday life.

———◆———

The direct outcome of meditation is calm, spiritual strength.

The power of reflection is deeper understanding.

August 24th

Reflection builds understanding, and with understanding comes wisdom. In reflection, you become more and more aware of the thoughts and behaviours that bring you happiness and those that bring misery.

In quiet reflection, your understanding of what really matters to you grows, and you come to realise that only by standing by those things will lasting happiness and peace be found.

———◈———

Through meditation, deeper understanding grows into wisdom.

Through perseverance, you grow steadily into your best self.

August 25th

Realising what matters in life and what doesn't is like lifting a veil to finally see the world clearly through fresh eyes. When it's your belief that the world is full of reasons to be negative, everything you see is filtered through that veil of negativity, effectively filtering any positivity out.

If it's your belief that nothing ever goes your way in life, you are filtering out everything that *is* going your way. If it's your belief that you will never find peace and happiness, you are filtering out everything in your life that would bring what you're looking for.

For as long as the veil remains in place, you remain set in your view of the world and set in your ways. Lifting the veil is opening your eyes and your mind to all that's around you and realising that you have *all* you need, it has just been hidden from view.

Believe that the life you long for is possible and it can be yours.

To achieve, you must believe.

August 26th

In all classic stories of good versus evil, there's a dark side and a light side. Whether it's the bad cowboy in the black hat versus the good cowboy in the white hat or Darth Vader versus Luke Skywalker, the two sides are polar opposites in every way. In the story of life, the dark side is represented by anger, pride, greed, vanity, envy, and hatred, while the good side is represented by gentleness, patience, purity, sacrifice, humility, and love.

It's not possible to be on both sides; there's no room in your heart for both dark and light, so which hat will you choose to wear?

———◆———

Where selfishness is, love is not; where love is, selfishness is not.

While you're looking out through selfish eyes, you will see no beauty.

To realise the best version of you it's possible to be, and to know in your heart that you are always doing the right thing, you must give up all thoughts and acts of selfishness. To be your best and do your best, and to find true happiness and peace, you must give up all negativity in your every thought and action.

Until there is no prejudice, unkindness, envy, hatred, or ulterior motive in all you think and do, there is always room for improvement.

Through selfishness you enslave yourself.

Let go of your selfish self and your best self can emerge.

August 28th

Peace is found in knowing your core values and in having full faith in your beliefs. What you believe to be true *is* true for you, but there is no peace found in pitching your beliefs against those of another. Stand firm and take comfort in what you know to be true, but allow others to do the same.

If you have certain beliefs, you can never look on your beliefs as being superior to those of another, and the same applies to differences in culture and ways of life around the globe.

True peace is not found in pushing your opinion on others; it can only be found in being your best, doing your best, treating all as equals, and treating others as you'd wish to be treated yourself. Perhaps then, through the fruits you reap, can you convince other of your way.

———◆———

In becoming your best, you are able to do your best for others.

Always being the best you can be and always doing the best you can do is perfection.

To succeed, an acceptance of the potential to fail is needed. However, accepting the possibility of failure is not the same as *expecting* to fail. Like change, failure is simply a part of life that must be embraced, and while expecting to fail is virtually a guarantee of failure, expecting never to fail is equally disastrous.

Strength is found in acceptance. In acknowledging the possibility, you mentally prepare for the eventuality, and there's no longer anything to fear. You accept that failure is not final, and you can learn from mistakes made and move on.

Expecting never to fail is failing to accept that mistakes may be made, thereby failing to take responsibility. Where no responsibility is taken, no learning can take place. To accept all eventualities is to be prepared to overcome all eventualities.

The cause of all power, as of all weakness, is within.

There is no progress apart from inner progress.

August 30th

Perhaps money is tight for you, and perhaps you're lonely and feeling pretty hard done by. You long for better days, but they never seem to come, and a dark cloud appears to follow you wherever you go.

Perhaps you complain bitterly, questioning why you've been handed this lot in life. Perhaps you blame the family you were born into, or the company you work for, or the powers that be for undeservedly handing you a hard life when someone else has been handed an easy life.

Complaining is not the answer, and being bitter will change nothing. The things you blame are not the cause of your hardship; the cause is within you. Only by identifying the cause will the answers you need to make changes for the better be found. They are also within you.

———⬥———

Orderly advancement of knowledge is the surest way to arrive at peace and prosperity.

In life, all is fair. There's no place for complaints of unjustness.

The thoughts in your mind colour and influence your reality. A wise man once said, "All that we are is the result of what we have thought. It is founded on our thoughts and made up of our thoughts." This means that happiness in your life is coming from happiness in your thoughts, and misery in your life is coming from misery in your thoughts.

But is it really this simple? Do outward circumstances have no influence on your inner thoughts? Circumstances can and do affect your thoughts, but the important thing to realise is that they can only do so in so far as you allow them to.

***

Your thoughts are your real self.

You are only swayed by circumstances until you understand the power of right thought.

September 1st

Mind over matter is not a cure-all for every physical condition, but a robust mind is needed for overall good health. A robust mind can overcome difficulties, find a way around things, and see positives rather than dwell on negatives.

Hypochondria is a well-documented psychological disorder, and it's known that those convinced of ill health will always find physical manifestations to add to their anxieties. With this being the case, the opposite is also true – the power of the mind can also promote good physical health.

Although not a cure-all, a healthy mind can be the fastest route to a healthy body, and in choosing to adopt a positive mental attitude, renewed strength can be found to overcome physical ailments. With positive thoughts, *all* negatives can be overcome.

———◇◇◇◇———

"A wise man should consider that health is the greatest of human blessings and learn how by his own thought to derive benefit from his illnesses." – Hippocrates

In choosing to put mind over matter, choose to put your mind to what matters.

"Money is the root of all evil" is a commonly used quote, but it's actually a misinterpreted quote. "The love of money is the root of all evil" is more accurate, but it's still a little misleading. Money in itself is not the problem, it's when money is valued more than people that it becomes an issue. When people choose to put the accumulation of wealth ahead of all else, greed makes it impossible to ever have enough.

Greed is the problem. A greedy person with wealth will stop at nothing to accumulate even greater wealth, and it's no different if the greedy person has no wealth, they will still put the desire for money ahead of any desire to do the right thing by others.

A greedy person with £1 million in the bank will consider themselves as poor as someone with no money because they want $1 billion in the bank. Poverty in the mind is poverty in reality because where there's no kindness, compassion, and love, there's poverty.

Money doesn't cause unhappiness, only the relentless pursuit of it.

A miser may be a millionaire, but they remain as poor as they were when they were penniless.

September 3rd

Anyone with the ability to harness the powerful forces of nature has formidable power, but anyone with the ability to harness the internal forces of the mind has equally formidable power. Not all forces of nature can be fully controlled, but gaining self-control, in your every thought and consequent action, makes you the master of your own destiny.

———◆◇◆———

The greater your self-control, the greater your knowledge and the greater your influence in the world.

The best use of knowledge is to increase the happiness of the world.

September 4th

For every cause, there's an effect. You can (and do) choose the causes you put into action, but you can't change the effects. You can choose what you think and what you do, but you have no power over the results of those thoughts and actions.

Once you have committed to an action, the result of that action can no longer be escaped. What's done is done, but all the power is back with you as you choose your next thought and action.

———◆———

All things, visible or invisible, are under the law of cause and effect.

Negative thoughts produce negative outcomes; positive thoughts produce positive outcomes.

September 5th

Think of life as a sum in arithmetic. Until you know how to do addition, there's no way of working out the correct answer. Once you know how it's done, working out the correct answer becomes simple. What once appeared as a complex and difficult task instantly becomes much simpler and manageable with knowledge and understanding.

In life, just like a sum, there are hundreds of ways it might be done wrong, but there's only one right answer once you know how it's done. With knowledge and understanding, the right way is found, and the way to solve every problem is known.

———◆◆◆———

Your power is limited by your conduct, and your happiness or misery is determined by it.

In life, as in arithmetic, a lack of understanding will always be revealed in the results.

September 6th

If life can be imagined as a huge piece of cloth, each individual thread in the cloth is an individual life. Each thread follows its own course and, although intertwined with others, it can only enjoy or suffer the consequences of its own making, not those of another.

In life, there's action and reaction, cause and effect, deed and consequence, and the counterbalancing reaction, effect, and consequence is always in ratio with the initiating action, cause, and deed.

———◈———

Selfish thoughts and ugly deeds will never produce a useful and beautiful life.

You make or mar your own life.

September 7th

For every action, there's an equal reaction, and this applies to thoughts every bit as much as behaviours. In thinking an unkind thought or in thinking of doing something hurtful to another, the hurt is instantaneous in your own mind.

Every little thought of unkindness brings a little more unhappiness into your heart and mind. In choosing to sink into a habit of unkind and hurtful thinking, you choose to sink into deepening unhappiness.

———◇———

You are responsible only for your own doing; you are the custodian of your actions.

An immediate happiness follows a kind thought or a kind action.

September 8th

The determination and commitment needed to see something through might be termed "willpower", and as such it's often mistakenly believed to be some sort of magical power that only a few super-human individuals possess.

For those who believe they don't have it, they look to others to support them and drive them towards their goal, but there's no substitute for self-motivation in terms of achievement.

Self-drive, the will to see something through, is not magical, it's readily available to all. The key to finding it is to apply it to every little task in everyday life. In establishing the habit of doing what needs to be done without putting it off until later, you are developing willpower. It's that simple.

Without strength of mind, nothing worth doing can be done.

The direct route to greater strength is to conquer weaknesses.

September 9th

Willpower can be developed by anyone. It's not mysterious, it's not complicated, and it can be achieved by following seven simple rules:

1. Break bad habits.

2. Develop good habits.

3. Give your full attention to the task at hand.

4. Do what needs to be done the moment it needs to be done and do it well.

5. Live by rules, don't just know the rules.

6. Control your tongue (think before you speak).

7. Control your mind (consider the actions your thoughts will influence).

Anyone who can earnestly reflect upon and practice the above will develop purpose and power of will.

In the development of will, the first step is breaking away from bad habits.

With willpower, you have what you need to cope with every difficulty and get through every emergency.

September 10th

Every change for the better made, no matter how small, is a change that's helping to develop willpower. The growing strength of will gained by successfully overcoming bad habits can be used to adopt good habits.

Ditching an old habit requires strength of purpose, and developing a new one requires redirection of that purpose, so there's no way around the need for disciplined effort. In other words, you can't take your eye off the ball.

———◆———

In giving in to a bad habit, you forfeit the right to rule over yourself.

In thoroughness, there's will; in shoddiness, there's weakness.

September 11th

Singleness of purpose is much more effective than trying to focus on multiple tasks at the same time. You might think you're multi-tasking, but unless you're putting your absolute best into each of those tasks, you're not achieving the best possible outcomes.

Give your full attention to the task in hand and do each task that needs to be done straight away. This might require a degree of prioritisation, but nothing should be put off until another time.

Adopting this attitude in *everything* you do develops a habit of doing, not procrastinating, and giving your best to everything you do ensures that the best outcomes will be achieved each time.

Perfection should always be the aim, even in the smallest of tasks.

Live according to steadfast principle, not what suits your mood.

September 12th

Lots of little things add up to big things. If you neglect any of the little things, you don't have what you need to create the big things. In realising this, you realise the importance of the little things.

If one little, seemingly insignificant aspect of your life is being neglected, it has an impact on everything else in your life. Taking time to reflect on what you believe to be the little, insignificant things in life can help you to see their significance in the bigger picture.

Thoroughness is doing little things as though they were the greatest things in the world.

With thoroughness, you acquire usefulness and influence.

September 13th

Thoughtlessness, carelessness, and laziness all add up to a job badly done. Unless you're putting thought, care, and effort into all you do, you're not putting in your best, so you're not going to get the best out of it.

As the saying goes, if a job's worth doing, it's worth doing well. Whatever it is you're doing, willingly do it to the best of your ability, and then whatever it is you want in life will come your way.

Lack of thoroughness is commonly caused by the pursuit of quick fixes and instant pleasures.

If it's instant gratification you want, the lasting pleasure of a job well done will never be yours.

September 14th

Thoroughness is completeness. Something done thoroughly has been done to perfection, or at least as close to perfection as is physically possible. In completeness, there's nothing left to be desired.

Everything that needed to be done has been done and done well. There's no completeness to be found in half-heartedness, and there can be no thoroughness where there's a lack of patience and perseverance.

———◈———

Where there's a lack of thoroughness in worldly duties, there's a lack of thoroughness in all things spiritual.

It is better to be a whole-hearted non-believer than a half-hearted believer.

September 15th

Despondency, irritability, anxiety, complaining, condemning, and grumbling are all indicators of wrong-thinking. These thoughts and accompanying emotions are often in response to the unhappiness and misery seen in the world, but in thinking this way, you are adding to it.

What's needed is right-thinking in the form of cheerfulness and happiness. You can do nothing better for the world than bring positivity into it, and avoid adding to the negativity – there's already enough of that.

Until you've learned how to be gentle, loving, and happy, you've learned very little.

Your surroundings are never against you; they are there to aid you.

September 16th

It's hard to stay negative when you're surrounded by positive people; it's hard to stay angry when you're surrounded by peaceful people; and it's hard to be unhappy when you're surrounded by happiness.

If you would have others be positive, be positive yourself. If you would have others calm their anger, be calm yourself, and if you would have others be happy, be happy yourself.

You can transform everything around you if you will transform yourself.

The way to true reform and peace of mind lies in living a life free of wrongdoing.

September 17th

If you are rushing through life in the busyness of one day to the next, it may be time to pause for a moment to consider what the rush is all about. What is it that you are trying to achieve? It's possible that you're working to achieve or maintain a certain lifestyle, or perhaps you're working hard to provide a secure future for your children, but if you step back for a moment, you might realise that you're living with an end date in mind.

In what way might your life be different if there was no end date? Irrespective of your religious or spiritual beliefs, imagine yourself as immortal. What would you do differently if you had all the time in the world?

———◆◆◆◆◆———

Immortality is here and now and is not a speculative something beyond the grave.

There's no need for hurry when you're living in the now.

September 18th

In considering yourself as immortal, you can truly live in the moment – the now. With no thoughts of time and the race against it, you have no need for hurry. If your life is ruled by persistent thoughts of "do it now while you can" or "enjoy it while you can", you are setting yourself a time limit and creating a constant sense of time running out.

In thoughts of immortality, there's no rush, and there's no endpoint by which everything you believe to be important must be achieved. With this understanding, you realise that being your best and doing your best in the moment, the now, is all that's important.

Immortality is experienced in life.

When you live in the moment, you can achieve all you want because you have all the time you need.

September 19th

In imagining yourself as immortal, you are able to see what matters. It's not the possessions you have or the trophies you've won that you take with you through eternity, it's who you are. When there's no beginning and no end, all that matters is now, and who you are in each moment.

—⊰◈⊱—

Live for today, but live as your best self in each moment of each day.

In immortality, there is no beginning or end, just an eternal now.

September 20th

The problem with overcoming selfishness is that many choose to define selfish in a way that excludes them. If you are one of them, you *know* in your heart of hearts what it means to be selfish, and you know when you're being selfish in your thoughts and behaviour.

Overcoming self is not overcoming all that you are, it's weeding out the elements of you that lead to sorrow and strife, the negative qualities, leaving the good qualities within you, the selfless ones that bring happiness and peace, with the room they need to flourish.

In overcoming self, you discard the sorrow-producing elements and keep hold of the happiness-producing elements.

Overcoming self is weeding out your bad qualities and cultivating your good qualities.

September 21st

Temptation can be overcome with knowledge. Think of temptation as a place of semi-darkness and knowledge as a bright light to shine into it. In the semi-dark, you can't quite see what's there; you can't quite see the source of the temptation, but in shining the light of knowledge into it, all becomes clear. Knowing what it is that tempts you puts you in a much stronger position to overcome it.

<hr/>

To overcome temptation, you must discover where it lurks and where the weak point is through which it's able to sneak in.

To know your enemy is to overcome your enemy.

September 22nd

Temptation is not the thing that tempts you, temptation is your desire to have the thing that tempts you. Temptation, therefore, is not an outward object but an inward desire. When you understand this, you realise that there's nothing or no one to blame but yourself, and in taking responsibility, temptation can be overcome.

———◆———

All temptation comes from within.

Temptation is a state of mind.

September 23rd

Where there's goodness, there's no temptation. A good person will never steal, even if an opportune moment arises. A good person can't be tempted to overindulge, or be tempted to lose their temper, because in goodness, there's integrity, virtue, and self-control.

———✦———

Goodness is never tempted: goodness destroys temptation.

Temptation will reveal true character.

September 24th

In selfishness, the fear of losing all you have leaves you wide open to being injured, robbed, degraded, and trampled on because you've already injured, robbed, degraded, and trampled upon yourself. In selflessness and integrity, there's no fear of any of these things. You are free and above it all.

———◆◆◆———

With integrity, you rise above fear, failure, poverty, shame, and disgrace.

When you know you've done no wrong, there's no need to prove yourself innocent or defend yourself when faced with accusations because your innocence and integrity alone are enough to answer any hatred.

September 25th

Be glad when you're pressured and tried by others. Be thankful for the opportunity to stand by your principles and to demonstrate the strength of your integrity. No matter what, you will never give up on what you know to be right.

You'll answer hatred with love, and wrongs against you with compassion. It may seem for a time that the wrongdoer wins and you lose, but the law of justice will always prevail. As the right-doer, you are invincible, and you will always rise victorious.

———◦◦◦———

With integrity, wrongs against you can always be turned around in your favour.

With integrity, you can never be subdued by the forces of darkness, having subdued all those forces within yourself.

September 26th

To be mentally prepared for all eventualities, your mind must be free from confusion. Where there's doubt, indecision, and uncertainty, there's going to be difficulty dealing with any problems that come along. Eliminating confusion comes down to exercising your mind and strengthening your powers of reasoning.

———◆◇◆———

If you are unable to discriminate right from wrong, you effectively have mind-blindness.

Your mind, like muscle, is developed with regular exercise.

September 27th

Unless you're prepared to reflect on your thoughts and beliefs,
there's potential for confusion. If you don't question your opinions,
others will.

The more you analyse what you believe to be true, the stronger
and more powerful your beliefs become as they stand up to scrutiny.
Errors in thinking will *not* survive under scrutiny. Through reflection,
you sort right-thinking from wrong.

Where there's lack of thought, there will be confusion.

The thoughtful will find their truth.

September 28th

Belief is the basis of all action. Your beliefs influence your thoughts, your thoughts influence your emotions, and those emotions influence your actions. The beliefs that dominate your mind are shown in the life you lead.

Everyone thinks, acts, and lives in accordance with their beliefs, and therefore the way you choose to live your life indicates the nature of your beliefs. Two opposing beliefs can't co-exist in one mind, so it's one or the other – hatred or love, peace or strife, selfishness or selflessness, justice or injustice? Your dominating beliefs will always become evident in your actions.

———— ⊱⊰ ————

Belief is an attitude of mind that determines the course of your life.

Belief and conduct are inseparable, for one determines the other.

September 29th

If you get enraged over what you believe to be injustices, believe yourself to have been badly treated, or often comment on the lack of justice you see in the world around you, your conduct indicates that you believe in injustice.

You might not see it this way, considering the opposite to be true, but your attitude shows that you believe confusion and chaos rule the world, and it's this belief that keeps you in a state of misery and unrest.

Justice reigns. All that's called injustice is fleeting.

When you believe in justice, you remain calm through all trials and difficulties.

September 30th

The way you live and the way you conduct yourself under trying circumstances tell another all they need to know about your beliefs and the principles you stand for. It's always going to be one or the other: do you believe in the power of good or the power of evil?

———◆———

Every thought, every act, every habit is the direct outcome of belief.

If your belief in a thing ceases, you can no longer cling to it or practice it.

October 1st

Those who believe in all things good will live among those things. Those who believe in all things bad will live among those things. The thoughts you harbour, your attitude towards others, and your actions are the things that will determine which camp your heart lies in.

———◦—◦◦◇◦◦—◦———

You can't cling to something you don't believe in. Belief comes before action, so all you do is the result of all you believe.

There are only two beliefs that affect life: belief in good and belief in evil.

October 2nd

A thought, no matter how secret, has the power to influence an action. A wrong thought, if it's kept in mind and revisited from time to time, will grow in strength until one day it leads to what appears to be an out of the blue and out of character action.

It appears out of character because it was a thought process that was kept hidden, and although it appears out of the blue, the action may be the end result of a thought process that began years before. Any thought allowed to settle in your mind has the power to attract all it needs to support it until the day comes when an opportunity to act on it arises.

As the fruit is to the tree and the water to the spring,
so is action to thought.

All wrongdoing is the natural outcome of a wrong thought.

October 3rd

Every thought you harbour in your mind will eventually be revealed in
what you do – good or bad. Each thought is a seed planted in your
mind, and if it's tended to and cultivated, it grows into a blossoming
action. The only way to avoid wrongdoing is to prevent wrong
thoughts from taking root.

———◈———

*Be careful of the thoughts you allow to settle in your mind
because what you are in your secret thoughts today
will become what you do another day.*

What you attract will always be in harmony with your nature.

October 4th

As you think, you become. Your thoughts appear in your character, so as the thinker of your thoughts, you are the maker of yourself and your condition. If your dominant mental attitude is happy and peaceful, these positive conditions will follow you through life.

If your dominant mental attitude is miserable and hateful, these negative conditions will follow you through life. As the thinker of your thoughts, you have the power to change your life.

———◈◇◈———

As a being of thought, your dominant mental attitude will determine your condition in life: your life is what you make it.

Any limits on your thoughts have been placed there by you.

October 5th

Where a negative mind sees only injustice, a positive mind sees cause and effect. In a positive frame of mind, it's impossible to see yourself as unfairly treated because you no longer see injustice. You know that no one can cheat or injure you because you've stopped cheating and injuring yourself.

Whatever negative attitudes or behaviours others display towards you, you see these as the effects of a cause previously created by you – moral debts that you need to repay. In meeting hatred with compassion and anger with peace, you become debt-free.

———◈———

If negativity is the flower, pain, grief, sorrow, and misery are its fruits.

Justice and love are one.

October 6th

Just as a body is built of cells and a house is built of bricks, your mind is built of thoughts. Your character, just as the character of another, is a compound of different thoughts, adding meaning to the expression, "As a man thinketh in his heart, so is he."

Individual characteristics are fixed processes of thought, but they are not so fixed that they can't be changed. Character is built in the same way as a house, brick by brick. New bricks laid can modify a building, and new thoughts laid can modify a character.

———◆———

The history of a nation is built using all it does as materials.

With millions of bricks, a city is built; with millions of thoughts, a mind is built.

October 7th

Good thoughts wisely chosen and well placed are the durable bricks
that build a happy life. All good thoughts are useful bricks, and
positive thoughts of strength and confidence inspire the building
of a 'mind temple' that will never crumble away, providing lasting
comfort and shelter.

To build this temple quickly and efficiently, all useless bricks in the
form of old and unhelpful thoughts and habits must be cleared away.

———◆———

Each one of us is a mind builder.

You are the builder of yourself.

October 8th

Just as a strong house is built on four solid cornerstones, a strong and successful life is built on the foundations of four moral principles: Justice, Integrity, Sincerity, and Kindness.

If you ignore these principles and try to achieve success through injustice, dishonesty, and selfishness, you are destined to fail in the same way that a builder cutting corners and attempting to build a house without strong foundations in place will ultimately build a house that's destined to sink, crumble, or topple over.

The strength of a building is dependent on the strength of the builder.

Build your life like a master craftsman.

October 9th

When you build your life using ethical principles as the foundations, and you make those foundations as strong as possible by never straying from those principles in any thought or action, you will undoubtedly build a strong and successful life.

However, never straying means paying attention to every thought, word, and action in every moment of everyday life. Even a tiny discrepancy can become a crack that weakens the entire structure.

———◆———

It is a common error to assume that bigger things are of greater importance than little things.

The strength of every small detail adds up to the strength of the whole.

October 10th

In wanting to be your best and do your best, you aspire to living a better life. When you concentrate your every thought on finding this life, you are practising meditation. Without intense aspiration, there can be no useful meditation.

In other words, if you're prone to daydreaming and drifting without purpose, there's nothing aspirational to meditate on, and therefore nothing purposeful can be achieved. Lethargy and indifference are fatal to meditation and to finding the life you want.

———⬦———

Where aspiration meets concentration, the result is meditation.

Meditation is necessary to spiritual success and to living a better life.

October 11th

Through concentration on learning, you might become a genius, but to find happiness, you need to meditate and reflect. Through concentration on learning, you might acquire power in your field, but to find peace, you need to meditate and reflect.

The perfection of concentration is power; the perfection of meditation is wisdom. Through concentration, you acquire skill in doing things in life, but through meditation you acquire skill in life itself – in living right.

———✦———

Through aspiring to find happiness and peace, your attention is given to finding it in your every thought and action.

In meditating on living right, you become fully immersed in living right.

October 12th

If you're a newcomer to meditation, the time spent in actual meditation may initially be short, but the knowledge gained in each short spell of concentration and aspiration stays with you.

In this way, early morning meditation can set you on track to a meaningful and purposeful day ahead. Begin with a few short moments, and with practice, you become more advanced, and you then become stronger, calmer, and wiser in all you are and in all you do.

As people, we are thought-beings. Life and character are determined by the thoughts in which we habitually dwell.

Through meditation, you purify your heart with repetitive thoughts on pure things and then apply those things to your everyday life.

October 13th

By dwelling on positive thoughts, the habit of positive thinking is formed. Through positive thinking, positive actions are taken. Repeating those positive thoughts leads to repeating those actions until those thoughts and actions are simply who you are and what you do.

Through meditation, repeated thoughts become habit, making it possible to move from uncertainty to certainty and from restlessness in life to purpose and focus.

———◈———

Through practice, association, and habit, thoughts tend to repeat themselves.

Take care not to mistake daydreaming for meditation.

October 14th

The rich and poor alike suffer for their own selfishness. The rich are continually losing their riches, and the poor are continually acquiring them, so the poor of today become the rich of tomorrow, and vice versa.

Fear also hangs over the selfish like a dark shadow. Anyone making or holding onto gains by selfish force will always be haunted by insecurity and the fear of losing those gains, and anyone selfishly seeking material gains will always feel harassed by the fear of destitution.

———◆———

Selfishness derives from ignorance.

Each individual suffers by virtue of their own selfishness.

October 15th

Until selfish desires and selfish opinions are surrendered, you will remain a slave to both. Through meditation, you can identify where selfishness lies, then reflect on the effects these desires and opinions have on your thoughts, words, actions, and therefore your life.

In surrendering selfishness, you surrender self, leaving behind only the positive qualities of selflessness.

The spirit is strengthened by meditation on all that's meaningful.

Only by trimming away all that's meaningless can the truly meaningful be found.

October 16th

Ridding your mind and your life of all selfish motives is a day-by-day process. Some days you might stumble, some you might fall, but in quiet reflection each night, you identify missteps and failures and you keep going, taking all that you learn forwards with you as you step positively into the next day.

In overcoming selfishness, the loss of today will add to the gain of tomorrow.

Learn to distinguish between the real and the unreal, the shadow and the substance.

October 17th

Everyone has an opinion, but do any of them matter? Everyone's opinion may be different, but this doesn't mean that any one of them is correct. When it comes to being better and doing better, no opinion matters, not even your own.

Goodness is goodness, there's no debate. The principles of goodness, purity, compassion, and love are unchanging; no other input or opinion is needed. Opinions change, principles remain steadfast and true. As Plato once said, "Opinions are the medium between knowledge and ignorance."

———◈◈◈◈———

Wisdom is realising how many things don't require your opinion.

Stand firm on the principles you value. Opinions are not facts.

October 18th

In finding what truly matters in life, you find what's in your heart and you find your true self. You are no slave to passion, no servant to opinion, and no follower of any path that leads you away from what you believe to be true.

In knowing what matters, your truth is easily distinguished from all that's false, and you gain the wisdom you need to live your life accordingly.

Live by what's in your heart and not as a slave to opinion.

To not know what is changeless in your heart is to not know anything.

October 19th

Where there's ego, there's always the potential for humiliation. Only by letting go of all pride, selfishness, and vanity can true inner peace and happiness be found. Where there's no self, there's no fear of humiliation.

———◈———

Know what's in your heart, and you are free from all doubt and uncertainty in life.

Where self is not, there's peace.

October 20th

All things in life are yours to choose. The weak can choose strength, and they will be strong. The ignorant can choose knowledge, and they will be wise. The choice is always yours, and the responsibility for each choice is always yours.

What you choose tomorrow may be different to your choice today, but in taking responsibility, you make no excuses. Your life is your choice.

Life is more than motion; it is music. Life is more than rest; it is peace. Life is more than work; it is duty. Life is more than labour; it is love.

Life is more than enjoyment; it is goodness.

October 21st

Unrest, discomfort, and disappointment can never be overcome by looking for solutions externally. In the same way that going on holiday can never solve any of the problems you have in life because they will all still be there on your return, attempting to get over disappointments without addressing the real source will only lead to further upset.

The search for solutions must begin within. Unrest, discomfort, and disappointment have not been thrust upon you by the outside world, they are your chosen response to external happenings. Overcoming them means recognising them as your own, not someone else's responsibility, and choosing to change your attitude to bring about a change in your response.

***

In the search for goodness, find yourself first.

What's in your heart is what's in your world.

October 22nd

For as long as you are dwelling on the past or the future, you are missing the present; you are forgetting to live now. All things are possible now, and only now. There's no wisdom in saying, "

If I'd done things differently last week, last month, or last year, things would be better for me today," or in putting off until tomorrow what can be done today. Wisdom is recognising the value and importance of today, the only true reality. The past and the future are nothing more than empty reflections.

All power, all possibility, all action is now.

Wisdom is putting away regret, anchoring anticipation, and living now.

October 23rd

All that you would be and hope to be, you may be now. Perpetual postponement is all that stands between you and accomplishment. To be, you must do, and doing must be done in the now.

Just as you have the power to postpone, you have the power to accomplish – and to perpetually accomplish. Act now, and things are done: live now, and you are today all that you can be today.

———◆———

To miss today is to miss reality.

Life is the here and now, not the tomorrows and yesterdays.

October 24th

Tomorrow is too late for anything. If you are living for tomorrow, you'll fail today. If you are telling yourself you'll get up earlier tomorrow; you'll do without procrastinating tomorrow; you'll get out of debt tomorrow, you're failing to recognise the importance of today.

If you're not doing it today, why will tomorrow be different? Rise early *today*; do without procrastinating *today*; and stay out of debt *today*. If you're waiting for help to arrive tomorrow, you're waiting for the cavalry to arrive… and the cavalry ain't comin'.

———◆———

Don't tell yourself you'll be better tomorrow, be better now.

You can only act in today.

October 25th

Leave what has not yet arrived and focus your attention on what is now. Concentrate on the moment and do all you can to ensure there's no loophole for regret to creep in.

When you choose to embrace thoughts of immortality, you no longer see your life as the time you have between the day of your birth and the day of your death. You become able to see that the birth and death of your body are not the beginning and end of a journey; they're just incidents along the way.

———————

In looking back to happy beginnings and forward to mournful endings, you're unable to see your immortality.

Everything in life and in the universe is now.

October 26th

To let go of egotism and self is to stop living life as a fragmented thing and to see all around you in the universe as a perfect whole – a circle of perfection. The circle is not contained in any form, but all forms are contained in the circle.

Radiant light is not captured in any one colour, but all colours are present in radiant light. In destroying all forms of ego, the simplicity of the whole universe and your part in it becomes clear. You are part of something much bigger than yourself.

───────◆───────

Put away egotism, and the pristine simplicity and beauty of the universe will be seen.

When you succeed in forgetting your personal self, you become a mirror in which universal reality is reflected.

October 27th

In knowing yourself, your understanding of others evolves. In understanding your world, you begin to stretch your understanding outwards to discover the universe beyond yourself and your world.

Only from a place of inner understanding can you begin to unfold and grow, and before knowing anything of a higher place or higher being, you must first know yourself.

In the perfect chord of music, each single note is indispensable, even though on its own it may be forgotten.

Cease to speculate about higher places and higher beings and know the all-embracing good within you.

October 28th

For as long as you refuse to give up greed, anger, jealousy, hatred, and opinions about this or that, you will remain at the bottom of the class in the school of wisdom.

To find knowledge, you must first find yourself and then realise that all of these negative traits are not you, they are simply what you're choosing to cling to. Let them go, and the real you is given space to shine through. There is goodness within you.

———⊰◈⊱———

Those who are pure and without vice know themselves as pure.

Purity is extremely simple and needs no argument to support it.

October 29th

Only the wise can comprehend wisdom, and those without it will argue that no one is wise. They will see patience, love, and compassion as weakness, meekness as cowardice, and wisdom as folly. Only the wise will see wisdom, and only the wise will refrain from passing any judgement on others.

———◈———

Goodness lives itself.

A blameless life is a truly wise life.

October 30th

In becoming the master of your own thoughts, the thoughts of others become yours. In knowing your own mind, you have no need to defend your thoughts, and you can instead mould the minds of others to match your thinking.

With goodness in your heart, you have what you need to transcend all problems, and the peace and patience it brings are all you need to win over the hearts and minds of the problematic.

In finding your true self, you have found reality.

Goodness and sincerity are one.

October 31st

In true wisdom, you see everything that happens to you as something useful. Everything happens for a reason, and everything that happens is utilised. Mistakes are noted as soon as they're made, and the lessons that can be learned from them are accepted and valued.

With wisdom, you know that there are no mistakes in the grand order of things, and through this understanding, you become wiser every day.

———◈———

In constantly seeking the approval of others, you will never find peace.

To love where you are not loved is a strength that will never fail you.

November 1st

Strength, wisdom, power, and knowledge can all be found within yourself, but they're not found in egotism, only in a willingness to learn. To learn, you must be willing to listen; willing to be advised; willing to learn from all experiences, and willing to take responsibility for failures rather than blame others.

Ego stands in the way of learning, and only by letting it go can you become better than you are.

———◈———

With wisdom, you are always keen to learn but never keen to teach.

The true teacher is in your heart.

November 2ⁿᵈ

Purpose is highly concentrated thought. There's no purpose in a half-hearted idea, and without purpose, an idea will never become a reality. Thinking you might lose some weight and get yourself in shape is half-hearted.

Planning to lose a set amount of weight each week, adopt a healthy eating plan and embark on a progressive exercise programme is purposeful. Thinking you might write a book is half-hearted.

Planning to sit down each day and write a set number of words is purposeful. It takes purposeful thoughts to drive purposeful actions, and where there's concentrated effort, there's accomplishment.

─────◆◇◆─────

Distraction is weakness; concentration is power.

All successful people are people of purpose.

November 3rd

In selfishness, you become a slave to doubt, anxiety, and worry. In selflessness, you become free. In choosing to free yourself from all negativities, you become open to all positivity – you become one with love.

In letting go of ego, you claim nothing, so you suffer no loss; you seek no pleasure, so you find no grief, and in being all you can be and doing all you can for others, you live a life of peace and happiness.

Know this – you make and unmake yourself.

You are a slave if you choose to be, and a master if you will make yourself one.

November 4th

Just as there's strength in a mountain, there's strength in patience.
A mountain can be formidable, standing up to the fiercest of storms
and yet also protective, shielding a newborn lamb.

Patience in a person gives them the strength to weather any storm of
criticism or harsh words, and also be gentle and kind towards others.
As glorious as the mountain is in its silent might, so is patience in you.

———◄●◆●►———

In patience, there's goodness.

In patience, you acknowledge your inner goodness.

November 5th

In today's 'bigger is better' world, having more is promoted constantly and being larger than life is applauded. Loudness and over-the-top confidence appear to be more appealing than quietness and humbleness, and getting ahead in life has become synonymous with getting yourself seen and heard.

However, "the bigger they are the harder they fall" is a saying that can be applied to this attitude. Where the self-promoters and applause-seekers fall, the quiet and humble stand tall. The glory of noise dies down, but the glory of peace and gentleness never ends.

When you live in patience and peacefulness, you live without fear.

In times of trial, the gentle and patient stand while others fall.

November 6th

Thinking that you can be hurt by the opinions and actions of others and therefore must defend yourself against them is flawed thinking. If you're feeling hard done by or unfairly treated, the negativity in your thoughts only increases the negativity in your world.

If false words are spoken against you, the words themselves can't hurt you. The hurt is created by you in your response to them. False words have no power to hurt unless you choose to be hurt by them, and no power at all until you choose to defend them.

The opinions and actions of others have no power over you unless you give it to them by responding negatively. Choose not to power them. Instead, meet all negativity and hatred with love.

———◆———

In meekness you resist none, thereby you conquer all.

If you take all negativity out of your own heart, you'll see the folly of defending yourself against the negativity of another.

November 7th

A great mind will always be of great purpose; a drifting mind will always be without purpose. Throughout history, those who have moulded the destinies of humanity have been purposeful in all they think and do.

As the Romans created their roads purposefully and directly to take them from point to point with no meandering, be purposeful in your thoughts and actions as you follow your own path through life.

Great is the power of purpose.

The purpose of life is a life of purpose.

November 8th

If your life is miserable because you feel misunderstood, your attitude will hold you back. If you often change what you're doing to please others and win their favour, your behaviour will limit your potential to succeed. If you are forever in two minds over who you are and what you want to achieve in life, you will fail.

Success in life comes with purpose in life – a purpose fixed by you. When you have purpose, you're no longer affected by the misunderstandings of others or in need of the adulation of others as you follow your chosen path. With purpose, nothing stands in your way.

Difficulties, mistakes, or any form of failure are simply steps that you are taking in your stride as you progress on your journey to success.

───◆───

With singleness of purpose, you can achieve anything.

Intensity of purpose increases in line with the number of obstacles faced.

November 9th

Anyone prone to shirking, always looking for the easy way rather than knuckling down and putting in the necessary effort, will always be uneasy in their mind. A sense of shame and loss of self-respect will hang over them. Historian and philosopher Thomas Carlyle once said, "He who will not work according to his faculty, let him perish according to his necessity."

In other words, if you don't use it, you lose it. If you don't use your muscles, you lose physical strength, and if you don't use your brain, you lose brainpower. Life and action are synonymous. The moment you choose to avoid necessary exertion, whether physical or mental, you begin your decline.

———⟡———

There is always joy in a task successfully accomplished.

There's no satisfaction like that of a job well done.

November 10th

Every successful accomplishment brings a sense of joy. A task completed brings satisfaction, and the more challenging the task, the greater the satisfaction. This applies to physical and mental accomplishments alike.

Just as the successful completion of a building brings immense satisfaction to the builder, overcoming flaws in character to establish new and better habits can bring immense satisfaction and joy to you.

———◆———

The price of life is effort.

The reward of accomplishment is joy.

November 11th

As you think, you travel, or where you look, you'll go. You are today
where your thoughts have brought you, and you will be tomorrow
where your thoughts take you. There's no escaping the results of your
thoughts, but you can learn from past thoughts and apply what you
learn to today's thoughts.

Your thoughts today influence your tomorrow. Dark thoughts today
take you to a dark tomorrow. Bright thoughts today take you to a
bright tomorrow. Thoughts can be altered, so you have the
power to alter where they take you.

———— ✦◇✦ ————

Everything that happens is fair and just.

*Nothing is fated, everything is form: your life is not fate,
it's your making.*

November 12th

Every aspect of nature contains a moral lesson. Learning these lessons brings wisdom. Just as seeds sown in nature will grow to become the plant they came from, seeds sown in the mind will grow to become more of the same.

Thoughts, words, and acts are seeds sown in life. In sowing hateful thoughts, you bring hatred upon yourself. In sowing loving thoughts, you are loved.

———◆———

Sincerity in your thoughts, words, and actions will bring you sincere friends; insincerity in you brings insincere friends.

When you know yourself, you will see that what you are is what is returned to you in life.

November 13th

Unless a farmer scatters his seeds on his land, there can be no crop. If he were to hoard instead of scatter, not only would the crop be lost but also the seeds themselves because they'd perish.

In sowing the seeds, he no longer has them, but those sown seeds bring far greater abundance into his life. The lesson to learn is this: In life, you get by giving. To hoard is to lose.

———◈———

To be happy, scatter happiness.

To find inner happiness, consider the happiness of others.

November 14th

If you are reaping bitter weeds of trouble, unhappiness, and sorrow, you need to question what seeds you have been sowing. Think of those seeds sown as your attitude towards others. Unless you sow seeds of kindness, compassion, and love, a crop of the same can't be harvested.

———◦❖◦———

What you reap is what you sow; what you give is what you get.

The way to obtain peace and kindness is to scatter peaceful and kind thoughts, words, and deeds.

In selfishness, false idols are worshipped. When these idols are material possessions, fashions, trends, and the opinions of so-called influencers, they are constantly changing. These things are not permanent; they're fickle whims, and they offer nothing meaningful or certain, and nothing that can be relied upon in life.

In selflessness, you're no longer ruled by ever-changing external forces. In selflessness, you have your true self and goodness to rely on. You know who you are and what matters most, and you know that you are unshakeable in your belief that true peace and happiness is found in doing all you can for others. In selflessness, you find meaning and certainty.

Selfishness is idolising yourself.

Selflessness is always doing the right thing for no other reason than you know it's the right thing to do.

November 16th

If you've ever been guilty of petty or selfish behaviour, you may well have been told to "get over yourself". Getting over yourself is getting to a place where you realise, understand, and accept that the world does not revolve around you. This is not always an easy place to get to.

To get there, you need to acknowledge that you may not always be right, that there may be a different point of view or a different way of doing things that is better than yours, and that the things you're choosing to get angry, emotional, or upset over may not be so important after all.

When emotions are high, it may not be a place you want to go to, but if you let yourself go there, you not only "get over yourself", you free yourself from the dark cloud of negativity that hangs over all selfish thoughts, words, and actions.

———◈———

Perfection is ready and waiting for all who earnestly seek it.

Get over yourself and you gain a life of freedom.

November 17th

If you want good things in life, you must do good things. If you want peace and harmony in life, you must think and behave peacefully and harmoniously. If you want fairness and equality in life, you must treat all around you as equals.

If you want to be better and do better in life, you must first understand what 'better' means to you, and then be and do whatever it takes to achieve it.

———◈———

Life doesn't change to suit you; you change to change life.

"You've always had the power... you just had to learn it for yourself." – Words of wisdom from Glinda in The Wizard of Oz.

November 18th

Until all selfishness is cleared away from your heart, there's no room for love of any kind (other than love of yourself) to come in. The longer you hold on to selfish thoughts and acts, the darker the great cloud of unhappiness that hangs over you becomes.

Love is available to all, it rejects no one, and it can be claimed and entered into now, this very moment, if you choose to make room for it.

There's no greater slavery than being at the mercy of your selfish whims.

There's no greater liberty than being free of selfishness.

November 19th

Is there justice or no justice in the world? The answer depends on your attitude and point of view. If you expect to see injustice, you'll see it everywhere, and if you're looking for justice, you'll see it everywhere.

Injustice is always seen through a veil of selfishness and negativity. In lifting the veil, a just world will become clear.

In all things, including thoughts and actions, there's perfect balance.

Happiness is mental harmony; unhappiness is mental inharmony.

November 20th

Selfishness keeps you blinkered to any other point of view beyond your own. If you choose to see yourself as a victim in life, being slighted, insulted, and hurt by others, then your focus keeps you firmly trapped in victimhood. The more you brood on your misery, the more misery you bring on yourself.

For every action, there is a reaction, for every deed, there is a consequence, for every cause, an effect, so until you choose to think differently and see yourself differently, believing yourself to be a victim means a victim is all you can be.

───◆───

You can never see beyond yourself until you choose to.

Justice cannot be seen by those engaged in conflict; light cannot be seen by those who choose to see darkness.

If you choose to stay in a state of resentment, you're choosing to inflict suffering on yourself. What goes around comes around. Living with resentment keeps resentment in your life.

For as long as there's hatred in your thoughts, there's hatred in your life; for as long as there's anger in your thoughts, there's anger in your life, and for as long as you keep bitterness and conflict in your thoughts, there's bitterness and conflict in your life.

———◆◇◆———

To understand cause and effect is to understand that what goes around comes around.

Ignorance keeps hatred and strife alive.

November 22nd

In finding goodness, you have put away all resentment, retaliation, selfishness, and egotism and arrived at a state of equilibrium. You now see ignorance and suffering on one hand and enlightenment and bliss on the other.

You see that both the oppressed and the oppressor, the robbed and the robber, the cheated and the cheat, all need equal sympathy, so in goodness, you extend your compassion to all.

———◆———

Cause and effect cannot be avoided; consequence cannot be escaped.

Unerring justice presides over all.

November 23rd

Think of reason as a torch that can be shone on your thoughts and actions to differentiate between those that are helpful and those that are not. There can be times when you feel you're in the dark, unsure which voice in your head you should listen to and which course of action you should take, and it's during those times that the light of reason is needed.

Perhaps one voice tells you that the selfish choice is best because if you don't put yourself first, who else will? The other reminds you that the selfish choice will lead to guilt and fear of losing what you gain, thereby keeping you in an equally dark place.

Without pausing to use the light of reason, erroneous choices might be made. Reason is in your heart, and through reason, you see the choices that represent right thoughts and right actions.

───◈───

Reason lights the way to seeing what's real and true.

Where there's no reason, there's error.

November 24th

Without self-control, there's no way of controlling all other elements of life. Self-control is self-discipline, and with discipline, there's purpose.

Those without purpose will drift through life, merely existing rather than living, but those with purpose live a life that has meaning. With discipline comes the power to mould your own destiny.

Without self-control, there's no life, only existence.

With self-discipline, you take control of your life.

November 25th

In the process of self-discipline, there are three stages: control, purification, and relinquishment.

Control: Self-control and discipline allow you to control all the moods and emotions that have at some point controlled you. You have control over temptation; control over those impulses that may have led to you spending money when you're meant to be saving, or eating cake when you're meant to be dieting, and you gain the power to bite your tongue, calm your temper, and thereby stay in control of yourself under all circumstances. With self-control, you can be your best self.

———◦◦◦———

"You have power over your mind – not outside events. Realize this, and you will find strength." — Marcus Aurelius.

In the heart of every man and every woman, there is a selfless centre.

November 26th

Purification: As self-control is gained, you are less and less swayed by temptations and more able to resist instant gratifications and fits of temper. However, restraint is only the beginning, the next step is purification.

In purifying your thoughts and actions, you're no longer resisting temptations when they arise, you're preventing them from arising altogether. You clear them from your mind completely by replacing them with good thoughts and good actions.

———◈———

Selflessness and self-control provide an inexhaustible source of strength throughout life.

Through purification, you find the strength to eliminate all temptation.

November 27th

Relinquishment: True strength, power, and usefulness are gained through self-purification. In relinquishing unhelpful thoughts, there's no wasted energy, and all of your energy can be put into generating helpful thoughts that will drive positive actions. With good thoughts at the helm, you can step calmly and purposefully forwards in your journey towards success.

———◆———

Eliminating temptation frees up thought energy to aspire to greater things.

Through purity, strength and goodness are developed.

November 28th

As your thoughts grow purer, you realise that all negativity is powerless unless you give it your attention. You now have the self-discipline to ignore it, turning your attention to developing patience, compassion, love, and wisdom instead. In so doing, you consciously embrace immortality, rising above all the uncertainties of life to live in unchangeable peace.

Self-discipline gives you the strength and purpose you need to step up to the next level.

Through self-discipline, you realise your true and best self.

November 29th

When you make a resolution, you are resolute, therefore determined to make something happen. This generally means you're unhappy with some aspect of your life and you're determined to make changes for the better.

With unwavering resolve, you will succeed in making those changes. If you're simply toying with the idea of possibly making some changes, you are not resolute in your thoughts, and those changes won't happen.

———⟡———

A life without resolution is a life without aims, and a life without aims is a drifting and unstable thing.

Resolution is the companion of noble aims and lofty ideals.

Half-hearted resolution is no resolution at all. Resolutions made hurriedly will most likely be broken as quickly as they're made. How many New Year resolutions have you half-heartedly made, and how many spur-of-the-moment resolutions have you actually seen through?

Take your time to form a resolution. Consider every detail of what it means and be clear on the difficulties you may need to meet to succeed. Only then, when you are mentally prepared for the challenges it brings, can you make up your mind to be resolute and to determinedly do whatever it takes to achieve your goal.

———◈◈◇◈◈———

True resolution is making it so!

Hasty resolutions are futile.

December 1st

Contentment is a state of happiness and satisfaction that comes with accomplishment. People that have accepted their lot in life might be described as being quite content with what they have, but true contentment is found in who you are.

Contentment is found in a job well done, not in a half-hearted effort; it's not found in giving up all effort, it's found in the sense of satisfaction and happiness that comes with that effort. Contentment is not resigning yourself to the life you have, it's feeling joy in the life you have – the joy of a purposeful life.

Indolence is the twin sister of indifference; planned action is the friend of contentment.

True contentment is the outcome of honest effort and purposeful living.

December 2nd

In true contentment, you're content with whatever happens, content with the people and things around you and content with your thoughts. To find contentment in these things means *not* being content with less than a best effort in all you think and all you do. Contentment is not giving in to what is, it's making what is the best it can be.

———◦◦◦◆◦◦◦———

In true contentment, you whistle while you work.

Results correspond exactly with efforts.

December 3rd

Community spirit, whether global or local, can't exist for as long as any one individual harbours selfish thoughts. Imagining a world without selfishness is perhaps an unrealistic dream, but it's not an impossible dream in your world. In choosing to be selfless in your thoughts and in your actions, you choose to put the needs of others ahead of your own.

In so doing, true peace and happiness become yours, and your thoughtfulness, compassion, and kindness will create a positive environment in which others around you are inspired to do the same.

Brotherhood, sisterhood, community... call it what you will; togetherness is what the world needs.

Where there's selfishness in one, there's no togetherness in all.

December 4th

From the spirit of humility comes humbleness and peacefulness; from self-surrender comes patience, wisdom, and true judgement; from love comes kindness, joy, and harmony; and from compassion comes gentleness and forgiveness.

In these four qualities – humility, selflessness, love, compassion – you have all you need to live a life that's free of malice, envy, bitterness, contention, and condemnation. You have all you need to live in a true spirit of togetherness with all others in your world and the world at large.

———◈———

True community spirit and togetherness must begin in each individual's mind.

Where there's pride, selfishness, hatred, and condemnation, there can be no true spirit of togetherness.

December 5th

In giving up ego and adopting thoughts of goodwill and peace, togetherness and true community spirit can grow. Togetherness is not just a theory or a slogan, it's a way of being and doing. For as long as you choose to look after No.1 and get into selfish arguments with others, there's no togetherness.

When you choose to be compassionate, to sympathise with others, and to see a different point of view, then your thoughts of goodwill and peace can bring true togetherness into your world.

Togetherness is created first and foremost by the abandonment of self.

In togetherness, your heart is at peace with the world.

December 6th

Before condemning another, take a good look at yourself. In what way do you believe yourself to be better than the person you're condemning? In demonstrating bitterness, resentment, and condemnation, are your thoughts and actions any better than those of the one you condemn? Consider all of this, and then try showing sympathy instead.

———◇———

Prejudice and cruelty become one and the same.

If you're prone to judging others harshly, try questioning where you may fall short yourself.

December 7th

To let go of past hurts is one way to begin growing in wisdom. Another way, and a better way, is to have no hurts to let go of. Any hurts you have in your mind are of your own making.

The only injuries you have are wounds inflicted by your own response to the attitudes and actions of others. When you take your pride out of the equation, you can no longer be wronged by another. Understand this, and you understand that a calm, wise, and hurt-free life is yours.

———◆———

Until dislike, resentment, condemnation, and all other forms of hatred are taken out of your heart, there can be no end to them.

There's no wisdom in being troubled by the wrong thoughts and wrong actions of others.

December 8th

For as long as there's resentment in your heart, you can't know peace. Peace is found in understanding that the wrongdoing of others comes from a place of ignorance.

With understanding, you know that the wrong attitude of others can't trouble you because understanding comes from a place of compassion and love, a place in which there is no room for resentment.

Being troubled by your own wrongdoing is keeping you on the right path to wisdom.

In living life right, you live in calm and wise understanding.

December 9th

The deeds and thoughts that lead to suffering are those that spring from selfishness. The thoughts and deeds that lead to peace and happiness spring from selflessly being and doing the right thing.

The process of switching from suffering to peace involves meditation and practice. In silent meditation and reflection, the answer to the question of what it means to be and do the right thing is found, and in putting those thoughts into practice, being your best and doing your best is accomplished.

The end of suffering and the beginning of peace is not found in the pages of a book; it's found in all you are and in all you do.

———◦✦◇✦◦———

Being your best and doing your best are the all-important things in living a good life.

The true meaning of goodness is not something that can be gleaned from a book; it can only be fully understood through practice.

December 10th

If you're prone to forcing your opinion of what it means to think, do, and live right onto others, or you find yourself engaging in arguments on the topic, you've missed the point of what it means.

Your opinion is of no consequence if what you're arguing for is not what you're doing. There's no right-thinking in telling others they must think as you do, and no right-doing in arguing the case for *not* engaging in arguments.

There's no right living in a "do as I say, not as I do" attitude, right living is all about what you think and what you *do*, not what you say.

———◈———

If you have goodness in your heart, you have achieved it through practice.

Only in a life of blameless conduct are you living right.

December 11th

Truth and love can never be the exclusive possession of any one religion, sect, or belief system. Any claim by any one organisation to have exclusive possession is a denial of love. Love is above and beyond and greater than any philosophy or opinion; love is all-inclusive; and love is deep enough and wide enough to envelop all; no one is excluded.

———◈———

Love must be all-inclusive.

Hatred is the absence of love, and therefore the absence of all that is included in love.

December 12th

The way of love is the way of life – immortal life. The beginning
of this way is the getting rid of all fault-findings, suspicions, and
disagreements. These petty vices are not love, and it's only by being
honest with yourself and in acknowledging them in yourself that you
can begin to make the changes needed to grow into love.

Only in learning to treat all others as equals, and with openness and
kindness at all times, can love become a binding principle.

---

*Love broadens and expands the mind until it embraces all in
kindness without distinction.*

Love is enlightenment.

December 13th

Wrong-thinking and wrongdoing bring unhappiness into the world. Right-thinking and doing can transform the world by bringing happiness. However, blaming the wrongdoings of others for your own unhappiness is not right-thinking.

Blaming others only brings more bitterness and hatred into the world. Your unhappiness is your doing, and only in understanding this can you find your own happiness. Only your thoughts and actions are responsible for your unhappiness or happiness, not the thoughts and actions of others.

———◈———

In living an enlightened life, all wrong-thinking and wrongdoing are abandoned, and right-thinking and right-doing are embraced.

Where there's finger-pointing and blame, there's no love, peace, or happiness.

December 14th

Irrespective of your religious or spiritual beliefs, everyone who has ever walked the path to betterment in life has travelled along the same ancient way as every great teacher before them.

Opinions, theologies, and religions may differ, but the journey to becoming your best self is the same for all. The ancient way to betterment is to be your best and do your best in every step you take and in every moment of every day.

———————

The principles of truth and love are fixed and eternal and can't be made or unmade by anyone.

Belief systems change from age to age, but the principles of virtue are eternally the same.

December 15th

In the teachings of all great teachers of every faith, the overriding
message is one of love. Throughout history and across the globe,
these teachers have all been influential in their wisdom, and all have
been a positive force for good. There might be many faiths,
but there is one shared love.

———◈———

One love; one world.

Great teachers are perfected flowers of humanity,
types of which all on earth shall one day be.

December 16th

Whatever your beliefs, you must never think of yourself as being on a "higher plane" than others. Being your best and doing the right thing in life is learning to see all people and all things as they are, never perceiving that they are somehow less than you are when what you see is different.

Your way is not the only way, and you must learn to put yourself in the shoes of another and see the world from a different point of view.

Goodness in your heart is freedom from all the cravings and indulgences of selfishness.

In life, as in McDonald's, go large with that – that being love and understanding.

December 17th

In changing times, the basic principle of divine justice brings a sense of certainty and security. Call it a spiritual law, a universal law, or call it what you will; divine justice is effectively the unchanging law of cause and effect.

Human justice can vary depending on the points of view involved, but divine justice is fixed. For every action, there's a consequence, an inescapable consequence.

———◈———

In adhering to the moral law, you find steady ground to stand on in an uncertain world.

Given the same cause, there will always be the same effect.

December 18th

Given the same thought or deed in a like circumstance, the result will always be the same. Without this ethical justness, there could be no human society. For every action, there's a just consequence, and understanding this provides fundamental certainty in life.

———◆———

All spiritual laws have the same infallibility.

The moral order of the universe cannot be disproportionate; if it were, the universe would fall.

December 19th

Having an understanding of and belief in divine justice provides certainty in life. Without it, there's no moral compass and no incentive to do the right thing. With certainty in this principle of justness, there's no room for chance, there's only unchangeable right. Whatever the cause, the effect will be just.

———◦◦◦◦◦———

Nothing can transcend what is right.

You can never suffer for something you have never done because this would be an effect without a cause.

December 20th

Characters, like plants, grow from seeds. The growth of a plant is a natural process of cause and effect, and so it is with character. A plant will flower according to its seed, and character will also flower according to the seeds of thought that have been planted in the mind.

Growth takes time, but as the flowers of genius and virtue appear, the mental seeds planted will become clear.

———◦◦◇◦◦———

Talent, genius, goodness, greatness; these traits are not given ready-made, they are the result of a long chain of causes and effects.

Nothing appears ready-made. There is always a process of changing, growing, and becoming.

December 21st

Think of your old, unhelpful habits and your new, helpful habits as two different countries. You can't live in two countries at the same time, so you can't live your life doing things the old way and the new way at the same time.

Moving from one country to another means leaving behind so much that's familiar, but unless those things are left behind, your new life in a new country can't begin.

In leaving behind old habits, you're leaving behind all the old and unhelpful thoughts and patterns of behaviour that kept you trapped where you were in life, and in so doing, you move into your new life with new and helpful habits that will free you to become whoever and whatever you want to be.

———◆———

An awakened vision calls us to a nobler life.

The sky is the limit when you shake your feet free from the weight of old mud.

December 22nd

With the right mental attitude, positives can always be found in every situation in life. With a positive outlook, lessons can be learned in every eventuality, and those lessons bring strength, knowledge, and wisdom.

Right thoughts are thoughts of courage, confidence, hope, and all things cheerful and happy, because these thoughts then generate right actions. With right actions, success follows.

———◦❖◦———

Right thoughts spring from a right mental attitude and lead to right actions.

Like a mountain climber reaching the summit, all successful people reach their success by positively thinking and working towards it.

December 23rd

The experience of pain teaches you how to be kind and compassionate. In knowing how it feels yourself, you gain a different perspective on how it feels for others.

Without this experience, you might say or do something that wrongs another and then think no more of it but having experienced how it feels to be the person wronged, you think differently.

For every action, there's a consequence. For every wrong thought and every wrong action, there's a corresponding consequence. The deed is not the end of it; it's only the beginning.

———◦⬥◦———

Failure and suffering are experiences that help you to learn and become better.

Through your own suffering, you learn to feel the suffering of others.

December 24th

The strong doing of small tasks leads to greater strength. No matter how small the task, doing it to the best of your ability will develop your skills and therefore your ability to do it more efficiently.

On the other hand, the weak doing of those tasks will lead to greater weakness. In other words, the strength or weakness of your character is seen in the strength or weakness of your behaviours.

In attaching value to all tasks in daily life, no matter how small, and giving them your best effort, strength of character is developed. In choosing to neglect small things and give them only a half-hearted effort, the squandering of energy only further weakens your character.

Every resource you need to be and do better is already within you.

The only way to strength and wisdom is to act strongly and wisely in the present moment.

December 25th

The past is in the past. Let it go and remember only the positive lessons learned. Let go of all thoughts of hatred, resentment, conflict, and ill will. Erase all memories of bitterness, grudges, and malice, and move on to begin a new day and a new year.

In this season of goodwill to all men, let your cry of "peace on earth" be truly meaningful by creating an environment of peace and happiness in your mind and heart.

———— ❖ ————

With each passing year, let its mistakes, hurts, and wrongs pass away forever, never to be remembered.

Have no wrongs to remember, no hurts to forget, and no hateful thoughts about others in your mind or in your heart.

December 26th

Instead of viewing difficulties as things to avoid, view them as useful stepping-stones in your journey towards being your best self. In this way, they're no longer things that get in the way of your progress, they're things that help you to keep moving.

Don't try to evade them: you can't. Don't try to run away from them: you can't, because wherever you go, they will still be there. Instead, meet them calmly and bravely. Weigh them up, get a measure of them, understand them, and through this understanding, you can overcome them.

Each difficulty overcome helps build your strength and knowledge, giving you an added advantage when the next difficulty comes along.

———◈———

There is no difficulty you can be faced with that you don't already have the strength to meet and subdue.

There's no peace in wrongdoing, no rest in error, no final refuge anywhere other than in wisdom.

December 27th

Consider this: what if the challenges that you think are sent to try you are actually sent because you need them? In whatever circumstances you find yourself tried, there must be a weakness in you, and it's a weakness that will remain unless you eradicate it. You need this trial to become stronger and wiser.

There are no circumstances that are trying to wisdom. Instead of brooding over your own trying circumstances, contemplate the lives and the trials faced by those around you. In contemplation, you'll find wisdom.

———❦———

Go to your task with love in your heart and you will go to it light-hearted and cheerful.

Think of the duty you shirk as your disapproving angel, and the pleasure you chase after as your flattering enemy.

December 28th

Little indulgences may be considered harmless, but no selfish indulgence is harmless. Every indulgence succumbed to is habit-forming. The more you indulge, the more difficult it becomes not to indulge, even when the initial indulgence seemed harmless enough.

Each time you succumb, the habit becomes stronger, and every bad habit formed is taking you further away from what matters in life.

There's no harmless indulgence.

Rise above impulses and indulgences, and you're no longer living vainly or uncertainly.

December 29th

Never meet hatred with hatred. If someone chooses to hate you, perhaps you said or did something that caused them to react this way. Perhaps there has been some misunderstanding, something you can smooth out with a little gentle reasoning, but whatever is said or done to you, never take offence and respond with more hatred. Instead, respond with love and understanding. Their hatred will be dissipated with love, but only strengthened if you add more hatred.

———◆———

You can end hatred by meeting it with love.

Open the floodgates of your heart for the inpouring of beautiful love that embraces all.

December 30th

Selfishness leads to misery, unselfishness to joy. This not only applies to your life but to the lives of everyone around you. Selfishness enslaves you, keeping you trapped. In letting go of selfish habits, you free yourself, but you also bring happiness to the lives of others.

In selflessness, you put the needs of others before your own, and in so doing, you find lasting peace and happiness.

———◆———

Enter the gateway of unselfishness to find abiding joy.

Aim for the highest good and you will taste the sweetest joy.

December 31st

Imagine the happiness of coming into a life of selfless joy from a life of selfish misery. Imagine the freedom of no longer being held prisoner by dark desires and no longer trapped in a never-ending cycle of hatred, anger, jealousy, and every other negative emotion. Imagine it, and then live it.

A life of peace and happiness is not just a dream, it's there waiting for you. Let go of the selfishness and negativity that's holding you back and step into a life of bliss and eternal happiness.
This happy ending is yours.

———————◆◆◆◆———————

There's no favouritism in the universe; all is fair and just, and each will be given their rightful earnings.

You can find the right way in life, and having found it, you can rejoice and be glad.

Final Thought

What feels like the end is often the beginning of something new.
Enter this new year with a gratitude for this new chance to create new
dreams. Let your *Daily Reflections* companion always be by your side
to help you aspire to become the best version of yourself.

My New Year's Aspirations

My New Year's Aspirations

My New Year's Aspirations

_____

_____

_____

_____

_____

_____

_____

_____

_____

_____

_____

_____

_____

_____

_____

_____

_____

_____

_____

_____

_____

_____

My New Year's Aspirations

_____

_____

_____

_____

_____

_____

_____

_____

_____

_____

_____

_____

_____

_____

_____

_____

_____

_____

_____

_____

_____

_____

_____

_____

_____

_____

Inspired by James Allen's *Book of Meditations for Every Day in the Year.*